THE ASSIGNMENT

ROSE MUGWE MUNGE

The Assignment:

90-DAY DEVOTIONAL

XULON PRESS

Xulon Press
2301 Lucien Way #415
Maitland, FL 32751
407.339.4217
www.xulonpress.com

© 2023 by Rose Mugwe Munge

All rights reserved solely by the author. The author guarantees all contents are original and do not infringe upon the legal rights of any other person or work. No part of this book may be reproduced in any form without the permission of the author.

Due to the changing nature of the Internet, if there are any web addresses, links, or URLs included in this manuscript, these may have been altered and may no longer be accessible. The views and opinions shared in this book belong solely to the author and do not necessarily reflect those of the publisher. The publisher therefore disclaims responsibility for the views or opinions expressed within the work.

Unless otherwise indicated, Scripture quotations taken from the New King James Version (NKJV). Copyright © 1982 by Thomas Nelson, Inc. Used by permission. All rights reserved.

Scripture quotations taken from the Holy Bible, New International Version (NIV). Copyright © 1973, 1978, 1984, 2011 by Biblica, Inc.™. Used by permission. All rights reserved.

Paperback ISBN-13: 978-1-6628-6762-0
Ebook ISBN-13: 978-1-6628-6763-7

Introduction

Growth is essential for every living thing. *"For the rain comes down and the snow from heaven and do not return there, but water the earth and make it bring forth and bud, that it may give seed to the sower and bread to the eater"* (Isa. 55:10 NKJV). It is the Sower's expectation that when he plants his seeds, they will grow and become food. It would be so discouraging to see seeds not fulfill their purpose.

Human beings are spiritual beings, and the Creator has a purpose for each of us. He wants to see growth in every area of life. Spiritual growth is essential, yet it's not seen with our physical eyes, and that could be why we don't pay much attention to it. Spiritually malnourished people are known by the way of their lives and how they relate with other human beings.

The Assignment is designed to help us in our spiritual walk, by daily encouragement, inspiration, and eye-opening scriptures. It provides the key nutrients that will boost the spiritual growth we all need to do and finish our assignments well. *"By this My Father is glorified that you [we]bear much fruit; so you will be My disciples"* (John 15:8 NKJV).

Keep this devotional close to you and feast on it daily. Your life will not be the same.

Rose Mugwe Munge

Day 1: The Party of Life

"Every man at the beginning sets out the good wine and when the guests have well drunk, then the inferior. You have kept the good wine until now" (John 2:10 NKJV).

It was at a wedding in Cana of Galilee. They were eating, drinking, and being merry. Celebrations went on for days, and they ran out of wine. This couple had invited Jesus to their wedding, so when they ran out of wine, Jesus came to their aid and solved the problem.

Many times, in life, we do not know who is seated next to us until we fall short of some things only, they can fix. This couple did not know the power Jesus had until they fell short of wine. Jesus used water pots of stone meant for the purification of the Jews. He only needed obedient people who could follow simple instructions. *"Fill the water pots with water"* (John 2:7 NKJV).

Are you in the party of life, and things are running out? Did you invite Jesus to this party? If you did, He will use His power to provide more than you can imagine. When we invite the Lord Jesus in our day-to-day lives, in case of any shortcomings, He will come through and fix our problems. He will make life meaningful and merrier.

What life situation are you facing today? Is it addiction, a life-threatening disease, relational problems, financial difficulties, or marital conflicts? Invite Jesus into your life today. He will fix the problem!

He calls for your obedience. What specifically is He telling you to do?

Prayer: Lord, I invite You into my life today. Take control of my life and help me to trust in you.

Day 2: I Hear the Chains Falling

"Suddenly an angel of the Lord appeared and a light shone in the cell. He struck Peter on the side and woke him up. 'Quick, get up!' he said, and chains fell off Peter's wrists" (Acts 12:7 NIV).

James, the brother of John, had been beheaded. Herod proceeded to seize Peter, and he was chained and put to jail.

There is daily persecution for those who boldly profess faith in Jesus. Yet there are times when Christians suffer in the wake of other people's sins. In Peter's case, he found himself in chains and was delivered to four squads of soldiers to keep him. The church prayed for him, and an angel of the Lord suddenly appeared and rescued him.

You might find yourself in chains today, chains of ungodliness, addiction, immoral living, and so on. There are people who have been praying for you behind the scenes. They have been calling you by name. *"The thief does not come except to steal, and to kill, and to destroy. I have come that they may have life, and that they may have it more abundantly"* (John 10:10 NKJV).

You might be going to church all your life but living in sins or bondage of some kind. What chains are still binding you? Are they chains of unbelief, the laziness of seeking God while He may be found, ungodliness, and filthiness before a righteous God? How long have you had them, and how much longer will you stay bound? The Chain Breaker is waiting and has the power to break every kind of chains. He is able to rescue you suddenly.

Prayer: Oh, Jesus, break my chains that I may be free and fruitful in the kingdom of God.

Day 3: Fix Your Eyes On Jesus

"Looking unto Jesus, the author and finisher of our faith, who for the joy that was set before Him endured the cross, despising the shame, and has sat down at the right hand of throne of God" (Heb. 12:2 NKJV).

"Some things are easily said than done." I am sure this thought has crossed your mind when you hear such Scriptures. That was me, and I still think it's hard to take my eyes off of the difficult situation of life and fix them on Jesus.

Jesus, on that night He was betrayed, *"was very sorrowful, even to death"* (Matt. 26:38 NKJV). In the following verse, Jesus said, *"O my Father if it is possible, let this cup pass from Me"* (Matt. 26:39 NKJV). It wasn't easy for Jesus either, but it was for this cause that He came to the world. He knew the Father's will, and He wanted to be obedient. Because of the joy that was set before Him, He was able to scorn the shame and endure the pain on the cross.

When the situations of life are so difficult and unbearable, fix your eyes on Jesus. He is the author and perfector of your faith. He knows and understands what you go through. In the secret and dark times of life, He can shine His light on them. There is no pain that can be compared to the pain He went through in our place. So, we can fix our eyes on Him, for He is watching and listening when we cry.

Prayer: Jesus, help us to fix our eyes on You. When it's so dark in our lives, help us to see the joy that You have set before us

Day 4: One Like the Son of God

"'Look!' he answered, 'I see four men loose, walking in the midst of fire; and they are not hurt, and the form of the fourth is like the Son of God'" (Dan. 3:25 NKJV).

Can you relate to this incident? Have you found yourself accused and punished for things you did not do? This happened to these faithful servants of God who would not bow down to the king's gold image that he had made. These men were ready to die for what they believed. They said, *"God whom we serve is able to deliver us from your hand, O king"* (Dan. 3:17 NKJV). Such boldness would only come from God and the knowledge of what He can do. Daniel continued to say that *"the people who know their God shall be strong and carry out great exploits"* (Dan. 11:32 NKJV).

What situation have you found yourself in? Is it at work where you are expected to do something against your beliefs? Or is it in your family setting or even pressure from within? Remember, *"The eyes of the Lord are upon the righteous, and His ears are open unto their cry"* (Ps. 34:15 NKJV). Stand firm and seek to do what is right, and leave everything else to God. He promises to be with you in the fire. Yes, He will be with you.

It is comforting to know from this passage that sometimes those who rage war against you will be the same ones who exalt you. They will join in singing your song, the song of praises to our God. The king finally said, *"Blessed be the God of Shadrach Meshach and Abed-Nego, who sent His Angel and delivered His servants who trusted in Him, and they have frustrated the king's word"* (Dan. 3:28a NKJV).

Prayer: Jesus, help me to always remember your promises for me: *"I will never leave nor forsake you"* (Heb. 13:5 NKJV).

Day 5: Who Can Separate Us?

*"For I am convinced that neither **death**, nor **life**, neither **angels** nor **demons**, neither the **future** nor **any powers**, neither **height** nor **depth**, nor **anything else** in all creation will be able to separate us from the love of God which is in Christ Jesus our Lord"* (Rom. 8:38–39 NKJV, emphasis added).

I have read this passage many times, and it has always been so encouraging and heart-lifting, and this morning, I went through each highlighted word and felt so loved. But when we go through hardships, this passage might not sound so true, but *"all the promises of God in Him are yes, and in Him Amen, unto the glory of God by us"* (2 Cor. 1:20 NKJV).

The chapter begins by telling us that *"there is now, no condemnation for those who are in Christ Jesus"* (Rom. 8:1 NKJV). The secret here is to be in Christ Jesus, giving ourselves to Him like He did when He gave Himself to us. He took with Him to the cross our condemnation, guilt, infirmities, pain, and sorrow and broke the chains so that we may go free. May you be encouraged today, knowing that the love our heavenly Father has for you is everlasting.

Like Job, sometimes those who see you suffering may condemn you, saying you might have sinned against God, and that could be the course of your suffering. It is true that *"all have sinned and fall short of the glory of God"* (Rom. 3:23 NKJV). But the work of Jesus on the cross blotted it all. So, the trials you go through now will not separate you from the love of God, which is in Christ Jesus our Lord. Give your life to Jesus, for that is where your friendship with Him begins.

Prayer: Jesus, help me to remember that even when things are very tough and it seems so dark, nothing will separate me from your love.

Day 6: **Abide In Me**

"Abide in Me, and I in you. As the branch cannot bear fruit of itself, unless it abides in the vine, neither can you, unless you abide in Me" (John 15:4 NKJV).

Have you ever taken time to see the interdependent relationship of the vine, branches, and roots? They all need each other; none of them can function without the other. Jesus likens Himself to a vine, and He calls us branches. His Father is the vinedresser. The vinedresser has the power to remove and burn the branches that are not bearing fruits. Once the branches are cut off, they wither and die. The remaining branches still attached to the vine bear many fruits.

There is a call to bear many fruits, and the only way is to abide in the vine. *"By this my Father is glorified that you bear much fruit; so you will be my disciples"* (John 8:8 NKJV). This is hard to comprehend, but that is the only way to go. Everything else will not bring glory to God. Going to church is good, and being in the choir and becoming a member is great, but all those are nothing if you do not have a personal relationship with the Lord. Once you have Jesus, who is the light of the world in you, many will see and desire to walk in your journey. You will be able to bring family members, coworkers, neighbors, and all those who interact with you to Christ.

The relationship between the Vine and Vinedresser gets even better because it comes with a promise: *"If you abide in Me, and My words abide in you, you will ask what you desire and it shall be done for you"* (John 15:7 NKJV).

Prayer: Lord, help me to abide in You all the days of my life.

Day 7: **Goodness and Mercies**

"Your goodness and mercies shall follow me all the days of my life. And I will dwell in the house of the Lord Forever" (Ps. 23:6 NKJV).

What a great comfort Psalm 23 is. It is the most known psalm, and many people quote parts of it so often. When I read it today, I saw a picture of my children when they were learning how to walk. They would start with small baby steps, and I would walk behind them with my hands wide open, just in case they would stumble and fall.

Like little children, God allows His goodness and mercies to keep following us throughout our lives. He is never tired of keeping this promise, and just in case we are scared of anything along the way, *"I will not fear no evil for You are with me. Your rod and Your staff, they comfort me"* (Ps. 23:4 NKJV).

The psalmist introduces the Lord and what He does for His sheep. He provides for and cares for His own. The first line of this psalm sums it all: *"The Lord is my Shepherd, I shall not want"* (Ps. 1:1a).

Dear reader, whatever it is that you desperately need, the Good Shepherd is able to provide. He understands what we go through each day. When we are hungry, He leads us to green pastures. When we become thirsty, He leads us to still waters. When we are heartbroken and have lost hope, He restores our souls. When we are discouraged, lonely, and abandoned, He sets a table right before our enemies. What a mighty God we serve. He understands our pain and sorrows because He lived a perfect life on earth as a 100 percent man and a 100 percent God.

Prayer: Help me to trust in You, for You know it all and care.

Day 8: I Am Doing a New Thing

"Behold, I will do a new thing, now it springs forth; shall you not know it? I will even make a road in the wilderness and rivers in the wilderness" (Isa. 43:19 NKJV).

If you are like me, there are times when life is so difficult and unbearable that we lose hope and become helpless. It becomes so dark; we do not know how the situation will ever change.

The chapter we are reading today has an encouraging message: *"When you pass through the waters, they will not sweep over you, when you walk through fire, you will not be burned"* (Isa. 43:3 NKJV). We wonder how true that is. We forget that He has promised to *"never leave nor forsake us"* (Deut. 31:8). Difficult situations make us forget that His eye is watching over us and His ear is listening to His children's cries.

He knows even before we get into difficult situations. Sometimes it's through our own doing, and at other times, we wake up on other people's sins. However way we get there, the Lord knows. And even then, His plans for us are good, and they do not cause us any harm.

Through His prophet Isaiah, God assures us that He is doing a new thing. Do you not perceive it, my brother and sister? He sure is making a way in your wilderness, wastelands, and hopelessness. Yes, He will make streams flow in your watch. Be encouraged, for He is faithful and has sworn by His Word.

Prayer: Lord, help my unbelief. Help me to wait on You because, in due time, You will change the situation I face.

Day 9: **Lazarus Is Dead**

"And I am glad for your sakes that I was not there, that you may believe. Nevertheless, let us go to him" (John 11:15 NKJV).

Being God, Jesus knew His friend was ill. When Lazarus' sisters sent a message to summon Him, it was not a surprise to Him. He got the message in time but decided to wait until Lazarus was dead. Why didn't He go right away to heal His friend?

The same case might be true for you today. You have prayed, fasted, and read the Word that says, *"Whatsoever you ask when you pray, believe that you shall receive"* (John 14:13 NKJV). You wonder, what else do I need to do? How else am I supposed to handle this situation? Our passage today says it is for our sakes that He has not come.

Finally, Jesus asked His disciples to join Him to go see Lazarus. His disciples questioned Him. "We should have gone while he was still alive. Why now?" My friend, Jesus wants to wait until you have completely lost all hope. He wants to come through when it is completely dark, so when He comes, His light will shine in the situation, and you will be able to tell that it was surely the hand of God.

There are two things I know: He will still come even when all hope is gone, and it will be at His own appointed time for your sake. Be encouraged, for He is surely coming.

Prayer: When all hope is gone, Lord, I will keep waiting upon You. Help me to *"trust and not be afraid"* (Isa. 12:2b NKJV).

Day 10: **This Is the Day**

"If they do not hear Moses and prophets, neither will they be convinced if someone rise from the dead" (Luke 16:31 NKJV).

Not many people can claim that they have not heard the gospel, at least not you. There are two books human beings can read about God's sovereignty: the book of God's words, the Bible, and the book of God's works. No human being in his right mind will miss one of them. The sun rises without fail and chases darkness, giving light to all creatures. Rain falls in small drops, *"making it bring forth the sprouts, giving seeds to the Sower and bread to the eater"* (Isa. 55:10 NKJV). He feeds all animals, big and small, on land, in the sea, and in the air. Mountains, valleys, forests, deserts, and seas are all in the book of God's works. It's then hard to miss the book of God's works. However, Christians have been commissioned to *"Go therefore and make disciples of all the nations, baptizing them in the name of the Father, and of the Son and of the Holy Spirit"* (Matt. 28:19 NKJV).

Most people have no excuse for not giving their lives to Jesus because they have it all. You have seen evidence of God in your life. Jesus said you might not be persuaded even if one rises from the dead. It is my prayer today that you take time to reevaluate you relationship with God.

Have you ever been convicted of your sin but did not consider giving your life to Jesus? Maybe at some point in your life, you have come to the verge of surrendering your life to Jesus, but when you think of all the things you still want to have control over, you shy off from the glorious call. You still have another chance. *"Today if you hear His voice do not harden your hearts"* (Ps. 95:8 NKJV).

Prayer: Father, I open my heart for You to come in and take control over my life.

Day 11: Reasoning Together

"Come now, let us reason together, says the Lord: though your sins are like scarlet they shall be as white as snow; though they are red like crimson, they shall become like wool" (Isa. 1:18 NKJV).

When I was little, I remember doing something terrible that called for severe punishment. I was so scared and not ready to face my father. I will never forget what my father did; he called me into the living room and talked to me in a way I could not have imagined. In my sinfulness, I felt love and compassion. My father gave me mercy and grace when I did not deserve it.

In our text today, the Lord of the universe has passionately and very lovingly invited us to reason with Him, "*for all have sinned and fall short of the glory of God*" (Rom. 3:23 NKJV). We deserve death as penalty for our sins. We cannot justify ourselves before a righteous God. Lovingly, He invites us to reason with Him. He has promised: "*though your sins are like scarlet, they shall be as white as snow; though they are red like crimson, they shall become like wool*" (Isa. 3:18 NKJV).

"*If you are willing and obedient, you shall eat the good of the land. But if you rebel you shall be eaten by the sword. For the mouth of the Lord has spoken*" (Isa. 1:19 NKJV). This a time of grace, and His arms are open wide for His children who turn to Him. He has promised to clean us up and help us start a new life. What is holding you back? Is it addiction of any sort, sexual immorality, or relational sins? What is keeping you away from the unconditional love of our Father?

Prayer: Lord, please "*create in me a clean heart, O God; and renew a right spirit within me. Cast me not away from thy presence; and take not thy Holy Spirit from me*" (Ps. 51:10 NKJV).

Day 12: **Do Not Quit**

"I remember, The kindness of your youth. The love of your betrothal, when you went after Me in the wilderness, in the land not sown" (Jer. 2:2 NKJV).

Do you remember that time when you first experienced that first conviction? All you wanted to do was give your life to Jesus. Remember how fiery you were and how you wanted to share the great news with everyone you interacted with? You wanted to share the good news even with strangers. You were unstoppable. What happened? After a short while, you became shy and not enthusiastic anymore. I know of a person who read the whole Bible within the first weeks of his salvation, but after a while, he stopped reading it regularly. Prayers stopped becoming a vital part of the day, and now, he only prays when something is wrong.

You are not alone. Many of us can identify with Peter's life. He is the one who walked on water like Jesus (Matt. 14:22–36) and cut the soldier's ear (John 18:10), but shortly after that, he denied Jesus three times before the cock crowed (Luke 22:54–62). It's very easy to judge Peter, and I wonder how he could so easily do that to our Savior. But if our lives were exposed and all the things we do daily, we would also be shocked. Maybe we would be embarrassed or cry bitterly like Peter.

In today's passage, God remembers those days that we used to be fired up for Him, and His good plans for us are still in place. Be of good cheer because this is the same Peter who Jesus said, *"You are Peter, and on this rock, I will build My church, and the gates of hell shall not prevail against it"* (Matt. 16:18 NKJV). Keep holding on, and *"being confident of this, that the good work that He began in you will carry it on to completion until the day of Christ Jesus"* (Phil. 1:6 NKJV).

Prayer: *"O Lord, revive Your work in the midst of the years"* (Hab. 3:2b NKJV).

Day 13: Obedience Is Better than Sacrifice

"This very day the noble ladies of Persia and Media will say to all the king's officials that they have heard of the behavior of the queen. Thus, there will be excessive contempt and wrath" (Esther 1:18 NKJV).

There is a time when we knowingly or unknowingly refuse to take orders from our superiors. At such moments, we never know the repercussions or impact of our actions. Our behavior sometimes might be due to our selfishness or brokenness. At times we simply don't honor the person giving orders, and we just choose to disobey.

In our text today, the king summoned his beautiful wife, intending to show off her beauty to his officials. On the other hand, Vashti, the queen, was hosting a party for the ladies and decided to disobey. The king became so angry and didn't know what to do. Memucan and the other officials said something had to be done; otherwise, *"there will be excessive contempt and wrath"* (KJV). The NIV says, *"there will be no end of disrespect and discord."*

Men reading this might be tempted to say that this is for women, but is disobedience only for women? Don't men disobey as well? This sin is in all mankind. It's found in children as well as adults, only at different levels. We never think our choices will affect others, but yes, our bad actions affect others as well. We are reminded that *"to obey is better than sacrifice. And to harken than the fat of rams"* (1 Sam. 15:22 NKJV). When we obey, we honor the person in authority.

We are also called to submit *"yourself one to another in the fear of God."* (Eph. 5:21 NKJV). By obeying or submitting, we show the fear of God in us, avoid conflict, and live in harmony at home, church, or even in our places of work.

Prayer: Help me to obey You and those in authority as my worship to You.

Day 14: **Courts of God**

"For a day in Your courts is better than a thousand. I would rather be a doorkeeper in the house of my God, Than dwell in the tents of the wickedness" (Ps. 84:10 NKJV).

Can you think of a ground that is solid and firm other than the foundation of Jesus Christ?

All things we seek to have or any place we desire to go can turn out to be a disappointment. We buy a dream house and put all metal bars to make it secure, then fire comes and consumes it. We buy big and good cars; they are involved in an accident, and we lose them. We work so hard and invest in stocks, but when stocks go down, we sometimes lose it all. The good health that we enjoy when we are young is only for a few years.

What remains forever? Is it fame, power, or wealth? Can any on the short list of things above give us peace and joy forever? We read of one kingdom that has *"inheritance incorruptible and undefiled and does not fade away, reserved in heaven for you"* (1 Pet. 1:4 NKJV). We need to work on this citizenship. This is where we will find perfect peace and real joy.

In the tents of wickedness are all sorts of pain and agony. Happiness is very short-lived if there is any. Are you stuck looking for peace, happiness, acceptance, validation, or satisfaction? You will not find these things elsewhere; they are only found in Jesus. He is the Prince of Peace, and His arms are open wide for you to come and find unconditional love in Him. He knows all of your needs and will not only give you rest but will also satisfy your hungry soul.

Prayer: Lord, help me to know You and find solace in You.

Day 15: **Redeeming Time**

"See then that you walk circumspectly, not as fools but as wise, redeeming time because the days are evil" (Eph. 5:15–16 NKJV).

When I was young, this didn't quite make sense, but as I advanced in age, I understood. Days have been evil since time immemorial, but they continue to get worse. The psalmist said: *"The days of our lives are seventy years. And if by reason of strength, they are eighty years. Yet their boast is only labor and sorrow"* (Ps. 90:10). We have a very short time here on earth, and we have assignments to complete. Yesterday is gone and cannot be recovered, and we are not assured of tomorrow. Today *"is the day that the Lord has made"* (Ps. 118:24 NKJV). Let's not only rejoice in it but do His perfect will.

We, therefore, cannot be procrastinators, for we don't know how much time we have left in this world. What the Lord has placed in our hearts, we need to do it and do it well. That word of encouragement that the Lord has placed in your heart, release it because it is not yours; it's meant for someone else. That word might save the life of a person contemplating suicide. The message of salvation in you should be shared. You never know how it might save a dying soul. If the Lord puts it in you to share resources, go right on. You never know who went to bed hungry.

Make a point of visiting a sick person in the ward or answering that call from a friend, relative, coworker, or neighbor. You could be the last person they talk to.

Kiss your kids and express how much you love them; you do not know how much time you have with each other.

Prayer: Lord, help me to live like I am on borrowed time.

Day 16: **Dangers of Idleness**

"Now it came to pass on the third day, when they were in pain, that two of the sons of Jacob, Simeon and Levi, Dinah's brothers, each took his sword and came boldly upon the city and killed all the males." (Gen. 34:25 NKJV).

When we have nothing worthwhile to do, the enemy brings evil ideas. And his mission is to *"steal, and kill and destroy"* (John 10:10). Dinah, Jacob's only daughter, had lots of time to herself. She decided *"to go see the daughters of the land"* (Gen. 34:1 NKJV). While she was in the city, the king's son spotted her and lay down with her. Her brothers were furious and were ready to take action.

Can anyone relate to this story? How do we deal with our boredom and idleness? How do we fill the empty space in us? What are the first things that come to mind for us to do? Is it gossip, illegal drugs, alcohol, sex, gambling? What is it? Do we think of how the choice will affect the people around us and ourselves?

In this chapter, you will find what pain and destruction Dinah's choice made to her family and the community near them. After the men were circumcised as per Dina's brothers' request, and were all so sore and couldn't defend themselves, Simeon and Levi were able to wipe away all men in that community, starting from the king to the youngest male. That which started as just a visit turned out to be disastrous. If Dina knew the outcome of her visit, maybe she would have considered otherwise.

Friend, *"There is a way that seems right to a man, but it's end is the way of death"* (Prov. 14:12 NKJV). Don't allow your mind to stay idle.

Prayer: Oh Lord, help me to find things to do that will glorify you when I am bored.

Day 17: **Repent**

"I will destroy man whom I have created from the face of the earth; both and beast, and the creeping thing, and the fowls of the air; for it repentant me that I made them" (Gen. 6:7 NKJV).

"*For just as rain and snowfall from heaven and do not return without watering the earth making it bud and sprout providing seed to sow and food to eat*" (Isa. 55:10). That is what we expect when we pray for rain. But God, who gives rain, chose to use it for other purposes. He regretted having created man because of his wickedness. God's anger was kindled, and He sent rain from heaven, and water also broke from the earth, killing every living thing and destroying all; tall and short buildings, cars, businesses, and anything else in which man had taken pride.

Oh, the sin of man and the damage it can course! There's nothing in this world that is of value than having a relationship with our Creator. All things – Jesus = Nothing. Nothing + Jesus = Everything.. He is the Almighty God, and He hates sin.

In His anger, He can use anything to eradicate it. He used fire during the wickedness of Sodom and Gomorrah (Gen. 19:24). He caused the ground to open and swallow Korah, Dathan, and Abiram and their children and their possessions (Num. 16). God can use anything to destroy sins.

If you have not yet given your life to Jesus, seriously consider doing so. God is faithful and will surely do as He intends to do. *"For behold, the day is coming burning like an oven and all the proud, yes, all who do wickedly will be stumble"* (Mal. 4:1 NKJV).

Prayer: Dear Lord, help me to heed your Word so that I escape Your wrath.

Day 18: **Blessed Is the Man**

"Blessed is the man who walks not in the counsel of ungodly, nor stands in the paths of sinners, nor sits in the seat of the scornful" (Ps. 1:1 NKJV).

I think this is a very powerful way of starting this book, a book that many people quote from. This verse touches obvious daily activities, but the way we do these things might bring us trouble and, in severe cases, death. Let's look at each one of them separately:

- Walk—Walking is very temporal. One doesn't walk for the whole day unless something is really wrong. Yet, this could be a life-changing activity.
- Stand—People stand for different reasons. Sometimes people meet unexpectantly and stand for a few minutes.
- Sit—People mostly plan to sit and do or discuss things or even sit to catch up.

All the above activities can change people's lives for better or worse. People go for prayer walks while others sit for Bible studies, yet others stand for worship. But people also walk, sit, and stand in bad companies, and sometimes they end up in jail because of the company they were in.

Our text today points us to a blessed man. It states that, that person does not do these things with the wicked. Think for a moment, how long does it take for a drug dealer to pass drugs to his customers? Who are you seated with, and what conversations are you having? Is it edifying or destroying you or someone else? *"Do not be deceived: Evil company corrupts good habits"* (1 Cor. 15:33 NKJV). Maybe all people need to see are the people you relate with, then they know the kind of person you are. How would you feel if the conversation you just had is brought to light?

Prayer: Lord, help us to remember that *"each of us shall give account of himself to God"* (Rom. 14:12 NKJV).

Day 19: Who Is Who in Your Life?

"And the things that you have heard from me among many witnesses, commit these to faithful men who will be able to teach others also" (2 Tim. 4:6–7 NKJV).

During Paul's ministry, he knew he would not live forever, so he intentionally took it upon himself to teach, train, and mentor Timothy. In his writing, he called him a son. Paul also had friends, Barnabas and Mark, who preached together (Acts 14–15 NKJV). They were missionaries together, and even when they had a disagreement and went separate ways, they reconciled and continued to spread the Word (Acts 15:39 NKJV).

In your life, do you have a "Paul," a person you look up to and one you would want to emulate and copy their ways of life? One who can teach, train, and mentor you, and one who can hold your hand through the storms of life?

How about a "Barnabas"? Do you have a true friend who can give you a shoulder to cry on? An equal partner in the ministry? One who does not judge you when you slip, and one who corrects you with love? Do you have a trusted friend you share your life with? One you can open up to?

How about a Timothy? Do you have one you are teaching, training, and mentoring? If not, why is that? The knowledge of God that you have should be passed on. If Paul did not train, teach, and pass on the gospel through the many letters he wrote while in prison, where would we be? You must pause for a second and think about who those three people are in your life. When you are no longer in this world, you will be sure the gospel will go on. *"To whom much is given, from him much will be required . . ."* (Luke 12:48 NKJV).

Prayer: Lord, help me to have a Paul, Barnabas, and Timothy in my life.

Day 20: Lose So as to Gain

"That I may know Him and the power of resurrection and the fellowship of His suffering, being conformed to His death, if, by any means, I may attain to the resurrection from the dead" (Phil. 3:10 NKJV).

Paul wrote the above text while he was in prison. Though it was written while Paul was in a very difficult situation, he constantly reminds us to rejoice in the Lord (Phil. 4:4). He counted as a loss that which a man would want to achieve in his days. He records all his achievements. *"Yet I counted all things as rubbish, that I may know Christ"* (Phil. 3:8). The only way that Paul could stand the torture in prison and still count it as joy was because he did not let his achievements get between his Savior and him.

I'm sure many people, including me, want to know Jesus as well, but the pleasures of this world keep coming between Jesus and us. We get trapped by the things we love and hold dear. It is hard to let go and not have them in our lives. The things Paul records as his achievements are not bad things. *"Circumcised the eighth day, of the stock of Israel, of the tribe of Benjamin, a Hebrew of the Hebrews: concerning the law, a Pharisee; concerning zeal, persecuting the church; concerning the righteousness which is in the law, blameless"* (Phil. 3:8 NKJV).

The above things blinded Paul, and he could not see Jesus. In the last part of the above verse concerning righteousness, he was blameless, and he said it was not righteousness that was found in Christ Jesus; it was according to the law.

If there is anything good or bad that would get between you and the Lord, please take time to give it a second thought. What is better than becoming a friend to the God of the universe and the King of kings?

Prayer: Lord, help me to count it all as rubbish so as to gain Christ.

Day 21: God's Ways Are Not Our Ways

"For My thoughts are not your thoughts, neither are your ways My ways," declares the Lord" (Isa. 55:8 NKJV).

He is unchangeable, unstoppable, unfathomable, not made by the hands of man, and He has no equal! He is God Almighty. We don't see Him with our naked eyes but see His wonderful works all around us. He is always at work and *"Even to your old age, I am He. And even to gray hairs I will carry you!"* (Isa. 46:4 NKJV).

On the other hand, the idols that are made by the things that our God created, after they have been made: *"They bear it on their shoulders, they carry it, and set it in its place, and it stands. From its place it shall not move. Though one cries out to it, it cannot answer, nor save him out of trouble"* (Isa. 46:7 NKJV).

I want a God who will carry me when I am weak and weary and have no more strength left, a God who will lift me up when I fall, and one who restores my soul when I am brokenhearted and have lost hope. I desperately need a God who knows all my needs and one who will lead me to greener pastures, and when I am thirsty, and the sun of this life is hot that I can't bear it, and when the noise from all sides of my life is so loud, I want a God who will lead me to quiet waters (Ps. 23:3-4).

Have you ever gone for an interview and become so hopeful, but then they send you a regret letter, stating that you did not qualify, but after a short time, you get hired for a dream job? What is mostly our first instinct when such things happen? We complain bitterly and fail to understand why things happened the way they did. May God help us to understand that: *"I make known the end from the beginning . . . My purpose will stand and I will do all that I please"* (Isa. 46:10 NKJV) and *"everything is working together for good . . ."* (Rom. 8:28 ESV).

Prayer: Dear Lord, help me to wait for You, for Your ways are perfect!

Day 22: **Lord, I Trust in You**

"You number my wanderings; Put my tears into Your bottle:
Are they not in Your book?" (Ps. 56:8 NKJV).

Thank you, God, for numbering my wanderings. That is an assurance that You, oh Lord, know my going out and my coming in. You know my every mental wondering. There's nothing that is hidden from You. You know: *"My enemies would hound me all day"* (Ps. 56:2), but you have always been on my side, taking note of all that I go through.

Thank you, Lord, for putting my tears in Your bottle. That tells me there's no heartbreak that goes unnoticed. Every pain, every sorrow, my Lord, you know. And it's not only knowing; You are doing something about it. There are times when I did not know if you ever noticed my mystery, but You always come through.

You remind me that when it is so dark, and I can't see You, You are still with me: *"The Lord is close to the brokenhearted; he rescues those whose spirits are crushed"* (Ps. 34:18 NKJV). Thank you, Lord, that You have also promised to be with me when I am in the valley: *"Your rod and Your staff, they comfort me"* (Ps. 23:4 NKJV). We would not ask to be heartbroken so that the Lord would be closer, nor would we ask to be in the valley so that the Lord would be with us, but it seems like the Lord responds to our cry and our struggles in life in a very passionate and personal way.

Whatever it is that you are going through, be encouraged, knowing that there's a God who is watching over you, and it's a matter of time before He will come to your rescue.

Prayer: Lord, thank you for being so intimate to the extent of collecting my tears in your bottle.

Day 23: **The Power of Praise**

"But at midnight, Paul and Silas were praying and singing hymns to God, and the prisoners were listening to them" (Acts 16:25 NKJV).

Humanly, we tend to think that when we are walking with God, everything will be perfect. Well, God sees things differently and sometimes allows trials and persecution to come our way with His good intentions.

In this passage, we see these two apostles praying and singing in prison. The other prisoners were listening, and the guard must have been listening as well. The Bible does not say if they got saved, but I am sure there were seeds that were planted in them.

Then there came an earthquake, the door flew open, and more miracles happened. Not only did the guard give his life to Christ, but his whole family did. They also got baptized in the middle of the night. We might not understand why hardships come our way, *"But so that the work of God might be displayed"* (John 9:2b).

What hardships have we found ourselves in today? Are we in chains of some kind? Have we tried to pray about it and nothing has happened? Praising God amid trouble is not easy, but the psalmist says: *"But You are holy, enthroned on the praises of Israel"* (Ps. 22:3 NKJV). He dwells right in the praises of His people. Therefore, whatever they ask, He provides because *"Every good gift and every perfect gift is from above, and comes down from the Father of lights, with whom there's no variation or shadow of turning"* (James 1:17 NKJV).

Amid hardships, pain, and sorrow, let's praise and worship our God. He has power to break our chains, set us free, and pave our way out.

Prayer: Though so hard, Lord, and very dark, fill my lips with Your praises.

Day 24: **Do You Have Anything to Say?**

"But when they hand you up, do not worry about how or what you should speak. For it will be given to you in that hour what you should speak" (Matt. 10:19 NKJV).

When we get in trouble, we worry ourselves out day and night, trying to prove our case, but it's comforting to know that the Lord knows our hearts and *"even before a word is on my tongue, behold, O Lord, you know it all together"* (Ps. 139:4). There's nothing hidden from Him. He knows our innocence, arrogance, and foolishness. You may have done it or not, either way, God is a *"Discerner of thoughts and intents"* (Heb. 4:12b NKJV). He is aware of how we got there. So, when they hand us over, He is able to turn things around for our sake. He is able to deliver you for His own name's sake.

God delivered His people in the days of the Bible. The apostles were handed over many times to the authorities for preaching the gospel (Acts 16, 17) and Shadrach, Meshach, and Abednego were thrown into the furnace (Dan. 3). He is the same God today and *"is able to do exceedingly abundantly above all that we ask or think, according to the power that works in us"* (Eph. 3:20 NKJV).

It might be so bad, but Jehovah God got this! Be faithful and do what is right, and leave everything else to God. Sometimes we suffer the consequences of our choices, and even then, God will give us strength to go through it. If they take us to jail, there's work for us to do there. Let's keep holding on, for He is still with us and in control.

Prayer: *"Though I walk through the shadow of the valley of death, I will fear no evil, for You are with me"* (Ps. 23:4 NKJV).

Day 25: I Lift Your Eyes

"I will lift up my eyes to the hills, from whence comes my help? My help comes from the Lord, who made heaven and earth" (Ps. 121:1–2 NKJV).

David had a very unstable life during King Saul's reign. He constantly ran for his life, for Saul wanted to kill him. There were times he and his men needed basic needs, but more so, they needed security.

In today's passage, we hear him asking the same question that we often ask ourselves: *Where does my help come from?* He lifted his eyes to the mountains. What is in the mountains? Some see mountains as a dwelling place for gods. They can also be viewed as places of refuge, but he did not find help from any of them. David finally found out that his help could only come from the Lord, the Creator of heaven and earth.

When trouble comes our way, to whom do we turn to? Do we turn to a spouse, family member, or someone who has a connection to one who can solve our problem? Where do you turn your eyes to? Who has been your source of help? *"Look at the birds of the air, for they neither sow nor reap nor gather into the barns; yet our heavenly Father feeds them. Are you not of more value than they?"* (Matt. 6:26 NKJV).

Jesus continues to tell us to *"consider the lilies of the field, how they grow without laboring or weaving . . . why worry about clothes?"* (Matt. 6:28 NKJV). He knows all of our physical, spiritual, emotional, and mental needs. He will make your *"enemies to flee before you seven ways"* (Deut. 28:7b NKJV).

Prayer: I lift up my eyes to You, where all my help will come from.

Day 26: **Road Map to Heaven**

"I am the way the truth and the life. No one comes to the Father except through Me" (John 14:6 NKJV).

Jesus said these words to his disciples, and today they are still very powerful. Jesus calls himself the way.

A few years ago, we used Google Maps to navigate our way to places. Then we advanced and started using GPS, and today we use our phones for navigation. If we put the address incorrectly, sometimes we might end up in a cemetery, and then the GPS will say, "You have arrived at your destination."

Jesus is the GPS of life that will never fail. The ultimate goal of our lives is to get to the place where he said, *"I go to prepare a place for you. And if I go and prepare a place for you, I will come again and receive you to Myself: that where I am, there you may be also"* (John 14:2–3 NKJV). Every single day and moment of our lives, we walk toward that goal. Though this journey is invisible, it is so real.

Jesus is also the truth. He wants His children to walk in truth because *"truth will always set us free"* (John 8:31–32 NKJV). Jesus has promised not only to be with us in the present journey of life, but He will also be with us as we cross the river of death and to eternity. Jesus conquered death and is alive forevermore. He said, *"I am the resurrection and the life. He who believes in me, though he may die, he shall live"* (John 11:25 NKJV). Do you have this hope?

Prayer: Thank you, Lord, for Your word that comforts, teaches, guides, and warns us as we continue in this journey of life.

Day 27: **God's Pavilion**

"For in the time of trouble, He shall hide me in His pavilion, in the secret place of his Tabernacle He shall hide me. He shall set me high upon a rock" (Ps. 27:5 NKJV).

Mostly, the pavilion I have in mind is a strong building, and you can't enter unless you are let in. The Scripture today is so comforting that during trouble, He will hide us in His pavilion. The verse elaborates what kind of pavilion it is; it's a secret place of his tabernacle. It is a place where we experience the presence of our God, a place of peace and great safety. He will surround us with his glory and love and set our feet high upon a rock.

Are you not glad that the God of the universe will come to rescue and hide you in a place where the enemy cannot reach you? During the storms of life, He will be your shield and shelter, and you will be safe in Him. If you fall and get stuck in a horrible pit, He will come to your rescue and take you to a resting place.

Where do you find yourself right now? Is it addiction, relational problems, physical or emotional pain? Or are you abandoned and lonely? *"Wait on the Lord; Be of good courage, And He shall strengthen your heart; Wait, I say, on the Lord"* (Ps. 27:14 NKJV).

The situation might not change much after prayer as we desire, but God will take us to a place of peace and calmness, where we can say: *"And now my head shall be lifted up above my enemies all around me, therefore I will offer sacrifices of joy in the Tabernacle. I will sing, yes, I will sing praises to the Lord"* (Ps. 27:6 NKJV).

Prayer: When the storms of life rage, when it is so grey, and we cannot see you clearly, Lord, help us to feel your embrace and unconditional love.

Day 28: It Shall Be Well

"Tell the righteous that it shall be well with them, for they shall eat the fruit of their deeds" (Isa. 3:10 NKJV).

God created Israel and chose them as His nation. He wanted them to be a role model of what God intended for His people in the world. Instead, they turned to the worship of idols, and everyone did as they pleased. God was displeased by their rebellion, and there were many times when He let other nations rise against them. Other nations oppressed the Israelites, which made them remember their God. In His infinite mercy, He would remember them and deliver them again and again through the judges.

Our text today is one of those times they had fallen short of God's glory. Things were tough, and again they cried to a merciful God. The passage is encouraging because it brings hope to the people. *"Tell the righteous it shall be well with them"* (Isa. 3:10a NKJV). That tells us that amid all the wickedness, God still had His remnant. He had those who had not defiled themselves. God also addressed the other group: *"Woe to the wicked! It shall be ill with him, For the reward of his hands shall be given him"* (Isa. 3:11 NKJV).

I do not want to be a judge over you, but I want to bring to your attention that there are two groups of people out there: the righteous and the wicked. By accepting the Lord Jesus Christ in your heart, He takes away your sins. He cleans you, and you can boldly say, *"He has clothed me with the garments of salvation, He has covered me with the robe of righteousness"* (Isa. 61:10 NKJV). So, when the righteous people are mentioned, you can count yourself in because *"the old has passed away, behold the new has come!"* (2 Cor. 5:17 NKJV). Where do you stand?

Prayer: Lord, thank you for your promise. I want to believe that it shall be well with me.

Day 29: **Secret Place**

"He who dwells in the secret place of the Most High shall abide under the shadow of the Almighty" (Ps. 91:1 NKJV).

We can choose to either dwell in the shadow of the Almighty or elsewhere. Then comes all the benefits of dwelling there. The psalmist said, *"He is my refuge and my fortress"* (Ps. 91:2 NKJV). The whole chapter makes it clear that by being in the presence of God, one is safe. Everywhere else away from the shadow of the Almighty is shaking ground. Away from the Lord is the dwelling of the enemy. There are the *"snare of the fowler; perilous pestilence; terror at night; arrows that fly by day; pestilence that walks in the darkness; destruction that lays waste at noonday"* (Ps. 91 NKJV).

We are living in a world full of uncertainties. As you can see from the paragraph above, there is so much that surrounds us, and it's dangerous everywhere. The battle is tough. *"For we do not wrestle against flesh and blood, but against principalities, against powers, against the rulers of the darkness of this age, against spiritual hosts of wickedness in the heavenly places"* (Eph. 6:12 NKJV).

Do you see why it becomes so tough that we cannot do it on our own? The only way out is to *"make the Lord, our refuge, even the Most High, your dwelling place"* (Ps 91:9 NKJV) and *"set your love upon Him"* (Eph.6: 14 NKJV). Then, the Lord will fight your battles. *"He will give His angels charge over you, to keep you in all your ways"* (Eph. 6: 11 NKJV).

The enemy might attack you physically, but your inner peace and joy will stay intact when you have made the Lord your refuge and fortress. This is possible by accepting Him in your heart as Lord and Savior by faith.

Prayer: Thank you, Lord, for making Your dwelling place available for me through your Son Jesus Christ.

Day 30: God's Favor

"His anger is but for a moment his favor is for life. Weeping may endure for a night but joy comes in the morning" (Ps. 30:5 NKJV).

It's very comforting to know that God's anger is but for a moment. That is so true based on the many times we fall short of God's glory. Every man and woman, even those who are in authority of the Word of God, fail, and we try so hard to do the right thing. *"But we are all like unclean thing, and all our righteousness are like filthy rags; we all fade as a leaf, and our iniquities, like the wind, have taken us away"* (Isa. 64:6 NKJV).

Yet our God, knowing that we can never achieve His standards, sent His only Son, who died for our sins, giving all those who believe and give their lives to Him by faith the garment of salvation and a robe of righteousness. His favor is for a lifetime. It's there for us to access through faith.

Because of His unconditional and everlasting love, He has invited us, saying, *"Though your sins are like scarlet, they shall be as white as snow; though they are red as crimson, they shall be as wool"* (Isa. 1:18 NKJV). Whatever you feel has come between you and your Creator, repent, and it will not be the same anymore.

Our own sinfulness have caused some pains. The pain of being disconnected from a loving Father, struggle with addiction, constant fights and conflicts, hopelessness, and all that is causing you to weep will be for only a moment because joy is about to come. Give this burden to the Lord by faith; He bore it for you at the cross and said, *"It is finished!"* (John 19:30 NKJV). Jesus completed the work of redemption, and all the prophesies in the Old Testament concerning Him came to pass. But it is also true that He brought to the end the bondage of sins, setting us free!

Prayer: Help me to believe that *"weeping may endure for a night but joy comes in the morning"* (Ps. 30:5 NKJV).

Day 31: **With You!**

> *"You are My battle-axe and weapons of war. For with you I will break nations in pieces; With you I will destroy kingdoms"* (Jer. 51:20–24 NKJV).

In today's Scripture, through his prophet Jeremiah, God was saying that He was about to do something in Babylon. He was bringing to pieces nations, horse and its rider, chariot and its rider, man and woman, old and young, young man and the maiden, shepherd and his flock, farmer and his yoke of oxen, governors and rulers, and all the inhabitants of Babylon and Chaldea (Jer. 51:20–24).

God is able to do all this breaking without any human help, just like He did during the floods when He saved Noah and his family or in times of Sodom and Gomorrah, when fire came from heaven. But He has chosen to invite and work with man.

Verses 20–23 start with: **With you.** It reminds me of Gideon, who tried to reason with God as to why he was not the right candidate for assignment. *"O my Lord, how can I serve Israel? indeed my clan is the weakest in Manasseh, and I am the least in father's house"* (Judg. 6:15 NKJV). Do you hear yourself in that conversation? Has there been a time when you felt that you are not worthy of the calling? In our eyes, we see the tall and strong, rich and famous, and eloquent and motivating as the ones God would use for certain works.

Today be reminded by the Word of God that you are the one God will use to accomplish His purposes in the world. *"For we are his workmanship created in Christ Jesus for good works, which God prepared beforehand that we would walk in them"* (Eph. 2:10 NKJV). You are not an accident in this world because *"Before I formed you in the womb, I knew you; Before you were born, I sanctified you"* (Jer. 1:5 NKJV). You were born with a purpose. God had you in mind before you were in the womb.

Prayer: Help me, oh Lord, to answer when you call.

Day 32: **Change Garments**

> *"So Jehoiachin changed from his prison garments and he ate bread regularly before the king all the days of his life"* (Jer. 52:31–34 NKJV).

God was angered by his people, the Israelites. He had seen them do it all: prostitute with the nations that worshiped idols, and His own chosen people burnt incense and gave blood offerings to the queen of heaven. In his anger, God gave them to Nebuchadnezzar, and they were taken captive and suffered all calamities that have been recorded in the book of Jeremiah.

Then Jehoiachin, king of Judah, was imprisoned, together with his fellow men. He had lost hope. All His majesty and splendor had been trodden on, humiliated, and put to prison like any other man.

One day, Evil-Merodach, king of Babylon, lifted Jehoiachin's head and brought him out of prison. *"And he spoke kindly to him and gave him a more prominent seat than those of the kings who were with him in Babylon"* (Jer. 52:32 NKJV). Jehoiachin changed his garments and ate in the presence of the king till he died.

What is going on with you today? What kind of prison are you in, and how did you get there? Was it by your bad choices, arrogance, and disobedience that you are in there? Either way, there is good news for you. The Lord is watching, and he will use evil men to rescue you from prison and set your feet in a palace. Then you must change your garments of shame, intimidation, and hopelessness and wear a new garment that will tell the world that you are not who they thought you were. You will wear garments of one whose life is changed, garments of victory and freedom.

You might be struggling with one area of sins and completely bound. There is good news for you; you can change your prison garments and enjoy freedom in Jesus's name.

Prayer: I do not know how, but I believe only You can change my life's situation.

Day 33: You Have the Final Word

"Who is he who speaks and it comes to pass, when the Lord has not commanded it? Is it not from the mouth of the Most High, That woe and well-being proceed?" (Lam. 3:37 NKJV).

Who among us has not gone through fire in his life? One would think that money is everything, but then things happen in life, and reality hits. There are things money cannot buy: good health, peace of mind, sleep, good relationships, favor, and so on.

For the Israelites, all had been taken away from them, including basic needs: food, shelter, and clothing. Their children cried for bread and wine, men were killed with a sword right and left, women were taken to captivity, and nothing was left behind; all these came due to their sinfulness.

The Israelites had forgotten their God, who had brought them out of captivity, and started to worship other gods. In his anger, God allowed the enemy to overpower them. He removed his hedge of protection that always surrounded and encamped their nation. The land was left desolate without beast or people. Even the temple of the Lord was invaded. Man's power and pride were quenched and reduced to nothing. In Lamentations, Jeremiah asked this so clearly: *"Who is he who speaks it and it comes to pass?"*

My friend, in the situation you are in today, only God has the final word. He knows how you got there in the first place, and only He, in His infinite mercies, can change and make things come to pass. He is Jehovah Jireh, Shammah, Nissi, Elohim, El Shaddai, El Roi, and so on. *"Christ is all and in all"* (Col. 3:11b NKJV). He knows what you are going through and understands your pain, and only he can patch all the pieces together to make you whole once again.

Prayer: Only Jesus has the final word. I will trust in Him.

Day 34: **Tie the Book**

"Now it shall be when you have finished reading the book the two shall tie a stone to it and throw it out in Euphrates" (Jer. 51:63 NKJV).

Sometimes, no matter what we do or say, there is someone who will hate and put us down. In today's text, the people of God had angered Him. They had forsaken Him and ran after other gods. In His wrath, He had sent them to captivity and allowed the enemy to trample over them.

The same God, full of love and mercy, saw the oppression of His people and turned against Israel's enemies. He had not forsaken His people. God told Jeremiah to read the Israelites' enemies' verdict, tie the book, and throw it in the Euphrates River, meaning, they *"shall sink and not rise from the catastrophe that I will bring upon her (them), and they shall be weary"* (Jer. 51:64 NKJV).

The love God has for His people is everlasting. *"For I am persuaded that neither death nor life, nor angels nor principalities nor powers, nor things present nor things to come, nor height nor depth, nor any other created thing shall be able to separate us from the love of God which is in Christ Jesus"* (Rom. 8:8–39 NKJV). God has promised to fight our battles, and He will not leave us alone. He knows our pains and struggles and is faithful to see us through. He is our judge, who is just; trust Him and do not take revenge. Let go and let God! He has His own ways of doing things that only He can do.

Prayer: Help me, oh Lord, to fully trust in You and let You fight for me.

Day 35: Not Me but Christ in Me

"I have been crucified with Christ: it is no longer I who live but Christ in me; and the life which I now live in the flesh I live by faith in the Son of God" (Gal. 2:20 NKJV).

That explains why true Christians are different from other people. They are unique and peculiar. They cry when other people around them are laughing and laugh when others are crying. The difference is found in this verse. *"Therefore, if anyone is in Christ, he is a new creation; old things have passed away; behold all things become new"* (2 Cor. 5:17 NKJV). The Trinity comes and dwells in them, and from there, their lives ought to change. They are led by the Spirit and do as He command.

I recently read an account of a Catholic monk. He learned how to dwell in the presence of God in all circumstances. On the outside, he was a poor, normal human being, but he was rich and full of the presence of God within. For that reason, he attracted many who wanted to experience God's presence.

Brother Lawrence was a dishwasher, the lowest occupation, and when he changed his job, he became a shoe repairer. He himself walked barefoot, but he repaired shoes so that others could walk more comfortably.

You might be in a very troubling situation and desire to have peace of mind but do not know how. Leaving our lives wholly to God makes us die to the evil things of this world and alive in Christ. We then can say like Paul, *"It is no longer I who lives but Christ in me."*

Prayer: Lord Jesus, will you please wash and clean me so that you find a place in my heart? I no longer want to live, but I want you to live in me.

Day 36: **What Is Left?**

"For the chewing locust left the swarming locust has eaten; what the swarming locust have left, the crawling locust has eaten; and where the crawling locust left, the consuming locust has eaten" (Joel 1:4 NKJV).

The people of Judah sinned against God, making Him full of anger. They had turned away from Him and started idol worshiping and sacrificing to other gods. Being the Creator of all living and non-living things, God can use anything He wants to accomplish His mission on earth. In this case, He chose to use locusts that ate every green thing, from leaves to the barks of trees, leaving the land desolate, with no food for man and the beast.

It is clear that God sent all kinds of locusts to do the work, which they did well. When God's people came to their senses and repented, our merciful God heard their cry. It's true when the Scripture says: *"If My people who are called by My name will humble themselves, and pray and seek My face, then will I hear from heaven, and will forgive their sins and heal their land"* (2 Chron. 7:14 NKJV).

Sometimes life can feel like there have been locusts of all kinds: the doctor states you have a terminal illness, you lose a loved one, a child is addicted, you get evicted from a place you have called home for many years, your car is repossessed, and so on. I do not want to say that sins have led to where you are, but what you may be going through could be a wake-up call.

Is there anything that you need to repent from? Humble yourself, pray, and seek His face because he is full of love and mercy. He is quick to forgive, change the course of our lives, and lead us to our destinies. He will show you his faithfulness by starting all over. There is nothing impossible with God. When life seems so dark, and there is no hope, fix your eyes on Jesus, for He alone can bring hope to hopeless situations.

Prayer: Oh Lord, I repent of my sins and ask You to take control of my life.

Day 37: **The Light of the World**

"Again, Jesus spoke to them saying 'I am the light of the world. Whoever follows me will never walk in darkness, but we'll have light of life'" (John 8:12 NKJV).

Jesus introduces himself as the light of the world and then tells us what would happen if we follow him. He says that those who follow Him will never walk in darkness. Then in Matthew 5:14, Jesus turns to His disciples and tells them they are the light of the world. In John 4:15, Jesus advises us to *"abide in Me (Him) and I [He] in you [us]."* If we abide in Jesus, He will shine through us, his disciples. There is no way that light will be missed by those around us unless we cover it with a bowl (Matt. 5:14). He has called us to carry out His mission in this world. In our day-to-day lives, Jesus expects us to shine His light in the very dark situations of our lives and those around us.

I know that as you read this devotional, you know of someone who is in a very dark situation in life. Some are about to face a jail term, those whose doctor's report has left them devastated and are wondering where they could find help, and those whose relationships are going downhill. Maybe a person you know is so depressed and about to commit suicide.

It's my prayer today that Jesus, who lives in us, will shine in those situations through us, his disciples. Take charge and boldly meet that person and encourage them; pray with them. When you obediently appear, the light of the world will be present and will shine in those people's lives. *"Let your light so shine before men, that they may see good works and glorify your Father which is in heaven"* (Matt. 5:16 NKJV). May that light be seen so clearly by all we interact with daily.

Prayer: Jesus, forgive me for the many times that my light has been dimmed by my sins, causing confusion and more darkness to those who hear me *"honoring You with my lips, but have removed my heart far from You"* (Isa. 29:13 NKJV).

Day 38: **Doing a New Thing**

"Behold, I will do a new thing. Now it shall spring forth; shall you not know it? I will even make a road in the wilderness and rivers in the desert" (Isa. 43:19 NKJV).

Dear child of God, *"Fear not, for I have redeemed you; I have called you by name; You are Mine"* (Isa. 43:1 NKJV). Sometimes this is all I want to hear. Hearing it from the King of kings and the Lord of the universe is more meaningful and has power in it.

Many are the times that we go through the fire of life; we wonder if morning will ever come. Everything seems to go wrong. I wonder what we do in such times. Habakkuk said: *"Through the fig tree may not blossom, nor fruit be on the vines; though the labor of the olive may fail, and the fields yield no food; though the flock may be cut off from the fold, and there be no herd in the stall—Yet I will rejoice in the Lord, I will joy in the God of my salvation"* (Hab. 3:17 NKJV).

I hope you are not like me; I complain when bad things come my way. I forget all the other times that God has come to my rescue. I fail to hear the voice of the Holy Spirit, my Comforter, as He tries to calm me down and assure me He is in control.

These very comforting words are for you and me. It may be so dark and hopeless, and you may have tried and come to the end of yourself. The Lord is asking you to observe with care what He is about to do. He is about to do a new thing! Brother/sister, don't you see it? He is about to do abundantly more than you can imagine. Rivers are about to flow in the desert and roads in the wilderness. Be of good courage and fix your gaze on Jesus.

Prayer: It doesn't seem like it's going to change, but I choose to believe Your Word, oh Lord!

Day 39: **Pursuit of Pleasures**

"Their sorrow shall be multiplied who hasten after another god"
(Ps. 16:4 NKJV).

Human beings have a vacuum within that naturally needs to be filled. The emptiness is caused by separation from our God, which was caused by our original sin. So, what we need is a Savior who gives us peace and fullness of joy. But when trying to fill the vacuum, we fall into many traps. Some have become big addicts of the things that once brought them happiness. Others have died in things they considered pleasures. Yet some have found themselves in prison for being involved in the things that are illegal.

"You shall not have no other gods before Me" (Exod. 20:3 NKJV). When anything fills the place of our God (money, drugs, sex, friends, name it), they become idols, and when we worship them, our sorrow is multiplied, and we are emptier than ever before. Nothing in this world can satisfy a hungry soul. No idol made by the hands of men or created thing like the sun or moon can satisfy. Only the one true God can! Only He who created man can satisfy: *"In your presence is fullness of joy; at your right hand are pleasures forevermore"* (Ps. 16:11b NKJV). True pleasure that is eternal is only found in the Lord our God, *"for He satisfies the longings of our souls and fills the hungry soul with goodness"* (Ps. 107:9 NKJV).

He created you in His image so you can have fellowship with Him. He is a jealous God and will not let you have peace until you give yourself to Him. *"The blessings of the Lord makes one rich, and adds no sorrow with it"* (Prov. 10:22 NKJV).

Prayer: Oh, Lord, help me to get rid of all idols that I might have, so as to be in your presence, where there is fullness of joy.

Day 40: **Living Hope**

> *"Blessed be the God and father of our Lord Jesus Christ, who according to His abundant mercy has begotten us again to a living hope through the resurrection of Jesus Christ from the dead"* (1 Pet. 1:3 NKJV).

Persecution has caused either growth and bitterness in Christian life. How we respond determines the results. Right and left, Christians are persecuted, whether in countries that have freedom of worship or not. Christians are often put down and ridiculed for standing for their faith. In such times, Christians can either grow in their faith or lose hope in their walk with the Lord.

In our passage today, Peter is blessing God and Father of our Lord Jesus Christ, who, according to his abundant mercy, has begotten us again to a LIVING HOPE through the resurrection of Jesus Christ from the dead, a hope to *"an inheritance incorruptible and undefiled and that does not fade away, reserved in heaven for us"* (1 Pet. 1:4 NKJV).

In our world today, we have defiled ourselves so much that we have defiled even the worship places. Fame, wealth, and other things that we chase every day soon fade away, and we do not have them anymore. Or we acquire so much through corruption, and then we fade away.

There is only one true living hope, and it is through our resurrected Christ. It is a sure hope, alive, and is not just a wishful hope; it is certain. In difficulty and the hopelessness of life, we know we can put our hope in Him. We can share that hope with people around us who are about to crash and commit suicide due to losing hope. If Jesus conquered death and resurrected, he can conquer and defeat our hopelessness and make us victorious, making us stand once again.

Prayer: Thank you for Your mercy that has brought us a living hope.

Day 41: Royal Priesthood

"But you are a chosen generation, a royal priesthood, a holy nation His own special people that you may proclaim the praises of Him who called you out of darkness into His marvelous light" (1 Pet. 2:9 NKJV).

Who is a priest? Our passage today says that we are a royal priesthood. Maybe it's easier to say we are of **a holy nation** and **special people,** and it is still very hard to convince ourselves that we are a **royal priesthood**; maybe we push that aside and leave it to the clergy.

The blood of Jesus has washed our sins away, and we are His ambassadors in this world. Jesus said, *"Go therefore and make disciples of all nations, baptizing them in the name of the Father and of the Son and of the Holy Spirit"* (Matt. 28:19 NKJV). The commission was for all who have received Jesus in their hearts.

The clergy have been added more responsibilities in the office of priests. They are our shepherds and spiritual leaders, and we should respect them. But we have to perform duties of a priest in our homes: pray, worship, and lead our family members to Christ. Share the good news with our neighbors and anywhere we may be at any particular time.

We are living in a very broken world, where many are overwhelmed with hopelessness. Suicide cases are surging, divorces are increasing rapidly, and orphaned children and widows are everywhere due to daily killings. What are we doing as Christians? It is also our responsibility to preach the good news because we have been "called out of darkness into marvelous light. We have been *"called out of darkness into His marvelous light"* (1 Pet. 2:9 NKJV). Are we carrying the light of Jesus with us wherever we go? Because if we do, *"Many will see it and fear, and will trust in the Lord"* (Ps. 40:3b NKJV). Do you know that we have been called to be part of the change in this world?

Prayer: Jesus, help us today to shine for You and chase the darkness in those around us. And help us to be priests in the world we are in.

Day 42: Generational Curses

"But Gehazi, the servant of Elisha the man of God, said, 'Look, my master has spared Naaman this Syrian, while not receiving from his hands what he brought. But as the Lord lives, I will run after him and take something from him'" (2 Kings 5:20 NKJV).

If only Gehazi knew the outcome of his greed, he would have had second thoughts. The disaster he caused his family and future generations was very severe, compared to the few perishable items he received from Naaman. If it were only him becoming leprous, that would have been an easier punishment. But for the curse to go to his future generations, that was tough. *"'Therefore, the leprous of Naaman shall cling to you and your descendants forever.' And he went out from his presence leprous as white as snow"* (2 Kings 5:27 NKJV).

This is very scary and hard to fathom, the things we do in secret without knowing that they will be exposed for all to see. Gehazi had been Elisha's servant long enough to see how powerfully God worked through Elisha. He would have asked, *"Please let a double portion of your spirit be upon me"* (2 Kings 2:9 NKJV), as Elisha had asked from Elijah. He should have asked something that would have had a positive and spiritual impact for all of his generations.

Choose to be faithful and walk in the light, and may integrity be your portion. Desire to be honest even when no one is watching. *"For nothing is secret that will not be revealed, nor anything hidden that will not be known and come to light"* (Luke 8:17 NKJV). If there's anything you did, and it's still a secret, REPENT! When people talk of generational curses, they never think that curses could start with them.

Prayer: Dear Lord, forgive all my sinfulness and do not let it be passed to my future generations.

Day 43: **Paralytic**

> *"And when they could not come near Him because of the crowd, they uncovered the roof where He was. So, when they had broken through, they let down the bed on which the paralytic was lying"* (Mark 2:4 NKJV).

Everywhere He went, our Jesus was doing good (Acts 10:38). He healed the sick, raised the dead, cast out demons, opened the blind people's eyes, made the dumb to talk, taught in the synagogue, loved on sinners, and many more. That is why it was very hard for the friends of the paralytic to bring the sick man to Him.

I can see their frustrations. Their friend was paralyzed, and maybe they had tried all doctors in the area, but there was no other hope left. Jesus was their last solution. They knew it was that day or never. The idea of breaking into someone's roof is mind-blowing. The houseowner's reaction was not their concern at that particular moment. Whether the wood up there was rotten or not, where they could fall did not stop them from pushing their agenda.

Finally, they let down the bed with the sick men. *"When Jesus saw their faith, He said to the paralytic, 'son, your sins are forgiven you'"* (Mark 2:5 NKJV). *"I say to you, arise, take up your bed and go to your house"* (Mark 2:11 NKJV). Did you note that the sick was healed because of the **faith** of his friends?

Have you ever taken on the burden of another person without counting the risks? Who in your family, neighborhood, church, or work place needs a bold move? Who, in their helplessness, needs to hang onto your faith? Are there people still struggling with sins around you? Won't you do something? *"Bear one another's burdens, and so fulfil the law of Christ"* (Gal. 2:4 NKJV).

Prayer: Jesus, give me a big heart and strong hands to help those around me.

Day 44: **Resume**

"Your servant used to keep his father's sheep and when a lion or a bear came and took a lamb out of the flock, I went out after it and struck it, and delivered the lamb from its mouth; and when it arose against me, I caught it by its beard, and struck it and killed it. Your servant has killed both lion and bear" (1 Sam. 17:34–36a NKJV).

I heard this story when I was a little girl in Sunday school class. You may have heard it around the same time as well. May it come alive in you today as we revisit it together. David, a young man, presented his case before King Saul. He put his resumé out there very clearly. He made Saul see he knew what he was doing. I don't think many had the same experience as David at his age. His resumé became even more seasoned when he said that the same God who delivered him from the lion and bear was able to deliver him from the hand of the uncircumcised Philistine. Please read the story again to refresh your memory.

The zeal and confidence David had for his God amazes me. He knew who His God was and what He could do. What are you facing today? Do you have giants you are so afraid of? What resumé do you have? Is there anything that your God has done for you in the past? Can you confidently say that the same God who saw you through things in the past is able to deliver you from the fears and situations you are facing today? The big question is: Whose name are you facing the situation with? Like David, if you are meeting your "Goliath" with the name of the Lord who fights your battles, you are on the right track because *"the Lord does not save with the sword and spear; for the battle is the Lord's and He will give [your enemies] into your hand*s (1 Sam. 17:47 NKJV).

Prayer: Oh Lord, bring to remembrance the things you have done for me in the past.

Day 45: **Killing the Anointed of the Lord**

"So, David said to him, how was it you are not afraid to put forth your hand to destroy their anointed of the Lord's anointed?" (2 Sam. 1:14 NKJV).

King Saul chased David for most of his youthful years, seeking to kill him. At some point, David was very close to Saul, who was in a cave. David cut a piece of his robe but spared the king. Then David said these to the king, *"My eyes spared you and I said I will not stretch out my hand against my lord for he is the Lord's anointed"* (1 Sam. 24:10b NKJV).

It's not easy to understand how one can spare an enemy who has been seeking to kill him for a long time if he was that close. David was truly *"a man after God's own heart"* (1 Sam. 13:14 NKJV). He respected the oil that was poured on Saul. He could have killed Saul, but he was the anointed of the Lord.

This is a challenge to the present world. It's not uncommon to find people who sue the Lord's anointed. It's not a problem for many to point a finger to the Lord's anointed. It's true that pastors and church leaders are not free from fault, but we still do not have any mandate to kill the Lord's anointed or even to point a finger to them.

Saul stopped chasing David, and he and his men went home. Although it's not clear when Saul stopped running after David, at least we are sure that after this particular time, he went home. We are advised to *"love our enemies and pray for those who persecute you"* (Matt. 5:44 NKJV). Is it an easy thing to love and pray for your enemies and those who persecute you? Absolutely not! But that's what we are advised to do. *"Vengeance belongs to me; I will repay, says the Lord"* (Rom. 12:19 NKJV). We can rest in that peace.

Prayer: Lord, help me when I meet my enemies. Give me a love for them and the strength to pray for them.

Day 46: Sojourners and Pilgrims

"Beloved, I beg you as a sojourners and pilgrims abstain from fleshly lusts which war against the soul" (1 Pet. 2:11 NKJV).

Our passage today addresses sojourners and pilgrims, people who have answered the call and started to follow Christ.

Our journey of faith is invisible but very real. Sometimes you might miss to check on the weather before you get dressed for the day, only to find out that the day turned out to be hotter or cooler, and the clothes you have on may not be appropriate for the weather. Yet there's nothing you can do, so you stay in those clothes until you get home. How about going out with shoes that are new but are stinging the toes, and you don't have any other pair? You keep them on until you get home!

Home is where you take off your jacket, tight or high-heeled shoes, and uncomfortable clothes. Home is where your joy should be complete. When we get home, *"He will wipe every tear from their eyes. There will be no more death or mourning or crying or pain, for the old order of things has passed away"* (Rev. 21:4 NKJV).

We have to conduct ourselves honorably so that *"when they speak against you, as evil doers, which they observe, glorify God the day of visitation"* (1 Pet. 2:12 NKJV). With our own strength, we cannot make it unless we totally depend upon God, and, therefore, we should constantly: *"Look unto Jesus, the author and finisher of our faith who for the joy that was set before Him endured the cross, despising the shame and has sat down at the right hand of the Lord of God"* (Heb. 12:2 NKJV).

Prayer: Dear Holy Spirit, constantly remind us that we are sojourners and pilgrims in this world.

Day 47: Sacrifices of Praise

"Therefore, by Him let us continually offer the sacrifices of praise to God that is the fruit of our lips giving thanks to His name" (Heb. 13:15 NKJV).

We have been called to continually offer the sacrifice of praise. I thought about "continually" and pondered for a minute; why must it be continually? Why not only when I go to church or when I'm happy and things are running smoothly? Just before my thought went afar, I saw this: *"How precious also are Your thoughts to me, O God! How great is the sum of them! If I should count them, they would be more in number than the sand; When I awake and I'm still with You"* (Ps. 139:17 NKJV).

The things the Lord has done to us, His thoughts about each one of us, are more than anyone could count. Sometimes we complain about the things that we go through, not knowing that if it were not for God, things would be worse. If it were not for God's protection, even when we are not aware, we would perish. We get tired and finally go to sleep, but He stays awake to protect us. He stays awake, watching over us. When we awake, He's still with us; when we are unconscious of the things that have weighed us down, He continually works for us; and when we come to our senses, He is still there with us. Hallelujah! Let's offer a continual sacrifice of praise to our God, for He cares and has good thoughts for us.

Also, *"Do not forget to do good and to share, for with such sacrifices God is well pleased"* (Heb. 13:16 NKJV). Whatever God puts in our hearts to share with other men, when we do it, that pleases our God. Share, therefore, the good news of Jesus Christ; share material things; and show the love of Christ in and out of season. The continuous sacrifice of praise and doing good and sharing with other fellow brothers and sisters pleases our God.

Prayer: May the praises of our great God be continually on our lips!

Day 48: Outside the Camp

"For the bodies of these animals, whose blood is brought into the sanctuary by the high priest for sin are burned outside the camp" (Heb. 13:11–13 NKJV).

The following three verses have "outside the camp" and "outside the gate." The sacrificial animal was killed outside the gate, outside the camp, then the blood was brought to the sanctuary to the high priest. When it came to God giving his only Son as the sacrificial Lamb, He was crucified outside the gate, and His blood and water that came from His head to toes went to the High Priest, God Himself, and the work of atonement was FINISHED! There were no more animal sacrifices. Jesus, the Lamb of God, became ENOUGH. He was taken outside the gate to be a reproach for us. Thank you, Jesus!

This day, for us to obtain God's mercy, we have to go outside our comfort zone and see the need for our Savior. He is gentle and loving and has done it all for us, but we have some work to do. We have to agree to come outside of the kind of life that we are in, which is not pleasing to God. We have to desire to come to Him to be washed of our filthiness. *"For the son of Man has come to seek and to save that which was lost"* (Luke 19:10 NKJV). He has already done what He needed to do for us.

The process of salvation has been completed. Jesus is now waiting for you to go outside the gate, outside the camp. There are things we love to do that are not pleasing to God: friends who influence us to sinfulness, addiction that has bound us for such a long time, hopelessness that is about to make us commit suicide, pain and bitterness that is so deep-rooted and causing physical pain, and so on. Get out of your comfort zone and come outside the gate: *"Come to me, all you who labor and are heavy laden, and I will give you rest"* (Matt. 11:28 NKJV).

Prayer: Thank You, Jesus, for bearing reproach for me. I am willing to come outside the gate and outside the camp to find You, Jesus.

Day 49: Do Not Fret

"Cease from anger, and forsake wrath; do not fret-it only causes harm. For evildoers shall be cutoff; but those who wait on the Lord, they shall inherit the earth" (Ps. 37:8 NKJV).

Easier said than done. How is it possible to see an evildoer, one who does evil without fear, who makes it known to everyone that he is doing bad things, and yet he prospers in all that he does? How easy is it to not fret when we trust God, who is the giver of all things, yet He doesn't prosper us? Is it possible to not fret when our children don't do well in school so that they don't get those good jobs, and whatever business they start, do not pick up?

Yet some people who are not walking with the Lord have everything they want. Psalm 37 is very encouraging, though: *"Do not fret because of the evil doers nor be envious, of the worker of iniquity. For they shall soon be cut down like the grass, and wither as the green herb"* (Ps. 37:1–2 NKJV).

Be encouraged and *"Trust in the Lord, and do good; dwell in the land, and feed on His faithfulness. Delight yourself also in the Lord"* (Ps. 37:3–4 NKJV). You have seen Him move mountains; He will do it again. He has rescued you many times, and He is not done with you yet. The evildoers are short-lived. Even when they outlive you, their lives end in this world. You are eternal; your new life starts after death. There is another life that has no end. So, *"Rest in the Lord, and wait patiently for Him; Do not fret because of him who prospers in his way, because of the man who brings wicked schemes to pass"* (Ps. 37:7 NKJV).

Evil men can apply wicked schemes, such as lies, corruption, stealing, killing, and doing other evil things to acquire wealth. But Christians have to be upright and wait on the Lord.

Prayer: Lord, help me to not fret when evildoers prosper. Please always remind me that *"A little that a righteous man has, is better than the riches of many wicked"* (Ps. 37:16 NKJV).

Day 50: Blame Shifting

> *"Then the man said, 'the woman You gave to be with me, she gave me of the tree, and I ate . . .' 'The woman said, 'the serpent deceived me, and I ate'"* (Gen. 3:12–13 NKJV).

Satan deceived Eve, *"You will not surely die"* (Gen. 3:4 NKJV), but see what happened. Sin brought separation between God and His people. They became ashamed of their actions and realized they were naked for the first time. After becoming guilty and ashamed, none of them was ready to take responsibility. They started to point fingers at each other. Adam blamed God for giving him the wife. He also blamed the woman for giving him the fruit. The woman blamed the serpent for deceiving her.

Does this sound familiar? Do you remember hearing these words as you were growing up? Is this something that follows you into your adult life? I see this all the time with married couples, and I remember learning that when a husband does not show love to his wife, the wife does not respect the husband. And so, each one blames the other for not doing the right thing. Then it becomes a vicious circle. Sometimes couples end in divorce, or they live a miserable life until one chooses to break the circle and take responsibility.

Is someone blaming you for their own sins? Or are you ashamed for what you have done, and all you do now is look for someone you can blame for what happened? If you have that urge to shift the blame, remember that it is sin that started with our original parents. That is why Jesus came to cleanse all of our sinfulness. Without shame, we can now own our sins and bring them to the feet of Jesus. *"If you confess with your mouth the Lord Jesus and believe in your heart that God has raised Him from the dead, you will be saved"* (Rom. 10:9–10 NKJV).

Prayer: Forgive me, Lord, for blaming others for my own sins. Help me to take responsibility and ask for forgiveness.

Day 51: Living Sacrifice

"I beseech you therefore brethren by the mercies of God that you present your bodies as a living sacrifice, holy acceptable to God, which is your reasonable service. And do not be conformed to this world, but to be transformed by the renewing of your mind" (Rom. 12:1–2a NKJV).

Different versions of the Bible have different wordings. ESV uses the word "appeal," NIV has the word "urge," and NKJV has "beseech." They are all strong in their own ways, but today I am inclining more to NKJV. I looked up the definition of beseech, and Wikipedia defines it as, "ask (someone) **urgently** and **fervently** to do something" (emphasis added). Immediately, my mind went to the verse in Ephesians 5:16, *"Redeeming the time because the days are [very] evil"* (NKJV).

Would you agree with me on this that the days are very evil? We have no time to waste; it's so urgent. Brethren! Present yourselves as a living sacrifice. There is no animal sacrifice that is done where the animal remains alive. He must die to get blood. We will present ourselves as dead animals to sin, like dead animals beside the road that do not hear and cannot act on any other vehicle that comes after it's hit and is dead.

That kind of sacrifice is *"holy and acceptable to God, which is your reasonable service"* (Rom. 12:1 NKJV). It is when we are dead to sins and the lusts of the body that the sacrifice is acceptable to God. The good thing is that if you have given your life to Christ, The Holy Spirit will tell you when you are conforming to the things of this world. You as a person have to intentionally cry to God for daily help on how you should be dead to sins. Let us seek to be *"transformed by the renewing of your (our) mind"* (Rom. 12:2b NKJV) because *"everything in the world-the lust of the flesh, the lust of the eye, and the pride of life- come not from the Father but from the world"* (1 John 2:16 NKJV).

Prayer: Forgive me, Lord, for the times I have conformed to the things of this world.

Day 52: **Oh Taste and See That the Lord is Good**

"Oh, taste and see that the Lord is good; Blessed is the man who trusts in Him! Oh, fear the Lord, you, His saints! There is no want to those who fear Him" (Ps. 34:8 NKJV).

It is true that most people, if not all, will try so hard to have a good life, which includes good health, a good home, a high-paying job, a big car, and so on. But to our disappointment, these things are good but do not satisfy the soul. There is still a vacuum that only God can fill.

We are invited to come and taste and see that the Lord is good. In food stores, they display samples for people to taste to see if they would like their new product. The idea is to make people buy it. It's not guaranteed that every shopper who tastes will buy it, but they expect people to have the awareness of the new product and buy it; if not then, maybe later.

The writer of this psalm also says, *"I sought the Lord and he heard me and delivered me from **all** fears"* (Ps 34:4 NKJV), fear of a pending ruling, report from the doctor, addiction in the family, relational problems, losing a job, death, and many other types of fears.

Have you tried to seek friends and relatives concerning some fear you have and then realized that they also do not have a solution? Try Jesus; He will never fail you. He will never leave you. He is saying to you: *"Fear not, for I am with you; Be not dismayed, for I am your God. I will strengthen you, yes, I will help you and have not cast you away"* (Isa. 41:10 NKJV).

The only fear that you need is of the Lord. Those and many more promises that He has made for His children make Him sweet and sweeter than the honeycomb. By faith, these promises are true and amen.

Prayer: Help me to taste and know that you are good, and that all of Your promises are true and amen.

Day 53: **His Workmanship**

> *"For we are His workmanship created in Christ Jesus for good works, which God prepared beforehand that we should walk in them"* (Eph. 2:10 NKJV).

We are created in His image for good works, which was prepared so that we should walk in them. Each of us, therefore, is designed for a good work. What is there for you to do was prepared beforehand before you were formed in your mother's womb, and it's God's good work that pleases Him when it is accomplished.

In Jeremiah, God is full of wrath because of the sins of His people. He allows the enemy to tear down their land, leaving everything desolate and taking men, young and old, into captivity. And all this time, He had His people at heart. He was waiting for them to repent to restore them. At some point He said, *"For Israel is not forgotten nor Judah."* (Jeremiah 51:5 NKJV) Sometimes it's hard to believe that God has not forgotten you when you are going through difficult situations. It helps to remember we are His workmanship, and He loves His work in us; together, we can accomplish much. In Jeremiah 51:20–24, it's written, *"You are my battle-axe and weapon of war. For with you, I will break the nation in pieces, I will destroy kingdoms: I'll break . . ."* (NKJV).

The Lord didn't just create and place you in this world without a purpose. You are his workmanship, and it's through you that He will accomplish His purposes into the world around you. God can do everything by Himself. He created heaven and earth and all that is in it by Himself and through the power of His Word that proceeded from His mouth. He is still very powerful and can do whatever He wants to do without our help, but He graciously wants to do things in this world through us, His workmanship. Seek to know what your purpose in this world is and then pursue and do it well.

Prayer: Help me to be a vessel that You can use to accomplish your purpose here on earth.

Day 54: **Apple of His Eye**

"Keep me as an apple of Your eye; hide me under the shadow of Your wings" (Ps. 17:8 NKJV).

How many times does an average person blink in a minute? Why do people blink? I would rather have you search for those answers. The truth is that the apple of an eye is one of the most protected parts of the body.

David is asking God to keep him as the apple of His eye. He is asking God to protect him as He would protect the apple of His eye. He, in the previous verses, cried to the Lord, expressing his innocence. He finds himself at no fault and, therefore, no need of being constantly on the run from Saul. He found out that his only resting place was in the Lord.

What are you going through, and for how long has that been going on? Has it been a prolonged time, as in the case of David and Saul? Or has it been from one thing to another? Have you sought for help here, there, and everywhere with no success? Is it a terminal illness? Is it barrenness, where the doctors have concluded that you will never hold a baby of your own? Is it rebellious children, and none of them is following the ways you brought them up in? What is it? Be encouraged, for *"The Lord is close to the brokenhearted and saves those who are crushed in the spirit"* (Ps. 34:18 NKJV).

You might not feel that closeness, but God's Word is true and amen. What He says shall surely come to pass. He sees all that you are going through, and He is so close to you, and like David prayed, He will protect you as one protects the apple of his eye. You are not alone in this. Keep trusting and believing, for, in due time, He will deliver you.

Prayer: Dear Lord, keep me as an apple of Your eye. Hide me under the shadow of Your wing.

Day 55: Son of Man

"And in the midst of the seven lampstands, One like the Son of Man, clothed with a garments down to the feet and girded about the chest with a golden band" (Rev. 1:13 NKJV).

There are many Johns in the New Testament. They have all done great things, and we learn so much from them. The John in today's text is also known as the Revelator. During the time of persecution, they tried to put him in boiling oil, but he did not die. They then decided to take Him to the Island of Patmos. *"I John, both your brother and companion in the tribulation and Kingdom and patience of Jesus Christ, was in the island that is called Patmos for the word of God and for the testimony of Jesus Christ"* (Rev. 1:9 NKJV). What was meant for evil turned out to be a great blessing to the body of Christ.

John was sent to this island to die there, but Jesus had other plans. He appeared to him and revealed all the things that we read in the book of Revelation. It was the best place for Jesus to reveal Himself to John. John was away from all distraction and was set apart for Jesus to use him in a way like never before. When you read the text, you will learn that John was afraid when Jesus was revealed to him, but he recognized who He was. He records that He was like the Son of God.

If Jesus appeared to you, will you be able to stand His glory and splendor? Are you in a situation that makes you feel like you are in an island? Have all the people you knew run away from you? Are you lonely? If you are right with God, take heart. Maybe this is the time Jesus wants to reveal Himself to you; the situation you are in might not be about you but about the body of Christ. Jesus wants to reveal to you about the seven churches and about the end time, which is for the edification and preparation of the bride of Christ. Stay faithful and, *"hold the beginning of our confidence steadfast to the end"* (Heb. 3:14 NKJV).

Prayer: Help me, Lord, to be faithful to You, even in dark times.

Day 56: **Burning Bush**

"And the angel of the Lord appeared to him in flames of fire from the midst of the bush. So he looked, and behold the bush was burning with fire, but the bush was not consumed" (Exod. 3:2 NKJV).

The verse that precedes says that Moses *"led the flock to the back of the desert, and came to Horeb, the mountain of God"* (Exod. 3:1 NKJV). When God wants to deal with us, His Spirit will lead us to undesirable places but on higher grounds with no interruptions. Moses saw a burning bush not being consumed. When he went closer, God spoke to him, but Moses started to argue with God. His fear of the past came between him and God. He was not ready to face tomorrow, yet he was in the very presence of God.

Two things hinder our service to God: yesterday and tomorrow; our mistakes and failures of yesterday and the fear of facing the unknown, sins that are still hidden under the rags. Moses had killed an Egyptian and hid the body under the sand (Exod. 2:12 NKJV). Worse even, God was sending him to the people who knew what he did. He was a wanted man! He once lived in Pharaoh's palace; now he had been a fugitive for forty years.

What past is messing up with your tomorrow? What unresolved sins still hold you hostage? Are you missing great opportunities because of things hidden under the sand? Fortunately, our God knows them all, and nothing can be hidden from Him. I am addressing those who are already at the mountain of God. The Spirit of God has already led you to His presence, but the hidden sins are tormenting and blocking you from answering God's call. *"This is the day the Lord has made; we will rejoice and be glad in it"* (Ps. 118:24 NKJV). Give your yesterday to Jesus; ask for forgiveness so that you can enjoy and rejoice in the day He has made and have the confidence to face tomorrow.

Prayer: Lord, always remind me that yesterday is gone and tomorrow is not promised so that I can face and enjoy the day You have given me.

Day 57: The Eye and the Ear of Our Lord

"The eyes of the Lord are on the righteous, and His ears are open to their cry" (Ps. 34:15 NKJV).

David wrote these words with confidence. He wrote this psalm after *"he changed his behavior before them, pretended madness in their hands, scratched on the doors of the gate and let his saliva fall down on his beard"* (1 Sam. 21:13 NKJV). What made David pretend? What would have happened if he did not pretend? David was in much trouble, and maybe this would have caused his death. However, David attested that during these very dark times, the eye of the Lord was always upon him.

His ears are open to His children's cry. He hears and turns His face to them. Hallelujah! *"Many are the afflictions of the righteous, but the Lord delivers him out of the all"* (Ps. 34:19 NKJV). Some afflictions are physical or terminal illnesses; there are broken relationships; we get fired from the only job that was the source of the family income; and long-term marriages are ending in divorce, and we wonder where our God is in such times. But the Word of God is very true. *"The eyes of the Lord are on the righteous, and His ears are open to their cry"* (Ps. 34:15 NKJV). Thank You, Lord!

There's nothing that goes unnoticed. His ears not only hear our cry, but they also hear all that people say about you. When they plot evil against you, our God hears! He comes and *"delivers us from the snares of the fowler and from the perilous pestilence"* (Ps. 91:3 NKJV). Today, like David, say, *"I will lift up my eye to the hills-from whence comes my help? My help comes from the Lord who made heaven and earth"* (Ps. 121:1 NKJV). Your help will not come from any other place; not from doctors, friends, therapists . . . Your help will only come from the Lord, the Maker of heaven and earth.

Prayer: Lord, You only *"have considered my trouble; You have known my soul in adversities"* (Ps. 31:7 NKJV). Father, deliver me from them all.

Day 58: In Your Presence

"You will show me your path of life. In Your presence is fullness of joy. At Your right hand are pleasures forevermore" (Ps. 16:11 NKJV).

Have you heard this phrase before? "As long as he/she is happy . . ." I have, several times. And those mostly considered to be happy are in a bad relationship, abusing substances, having affairs outside their marriages, and leading rebellious lives. *"There is a way that seems right to a man, but its end is the way of death"* (Prov. 14:12 NKJV). Happiness acquired in malicious ways are short-lived and end in sorrow.

The things we idolize and chase after do not end well. David writes, *"Their sorrow shall be multiplied who hasten after other gods"* (Ps. 16:4 NKJV. Children are born outside of wedlock, there is divorce due to selfish ambitions, and poor children are traumatized throughout their lives. People are caught up in love triangles, where death is likely the outcome. Others become addicted by the things that once gave them temporary pleasure and are bound for life.

In our text today, David makes it clear that it's in the presence of the Lord that he found FULLNESS of joy. I think most human beings need true joy and blessings that are added to no sorrow. That, dear friend, is only found in God. Only He can freely give without any strings attached.

Do not continue in pursuit of the wrong happiness that brings enmity between you and your Creator. *"Before I formed you in the womb, I knew you; before you were born, I sanctified you; I ordained you as a prophet to the nations"* (Jer. 1:5 NKJV). Have you tried to run away from the reality of life? For how long will you continue to be rebellious? *"At His right hand are pleasures FOREVERMORE"* (Ps. 16:11 NKJV). You need to run back to God, who gives pleasures forevermore.

Prayer: Oh Lord, help me to find the fullness of joy in Your presence and pleasures forevermore.

Day 59: **Go With Us**

"If Your presence does not go with us, do not bring us up from here. For how then will it be known that Your people and I have found grace in Your sight except You go with us?" (Exod. 33:16–16 NKJV).

These are the words of Moses while he was in the wilderness with the Israelites. They had left Egypt and had crossed the Red Sea, had seen Pharaoh's army perish in the Red Sea, and had seen God delivering them in a mighty way. Having seen all these, they had become a stiff-necked people. God wasn't going with them into the land flowing with milk and honey, *"lest I consume you on the way"* (Exod. 33:3b NKJV)

As Moses pleaded their case with God, he asked how Isrealites will go without His presence. From Egypt, they were known as God's people, and miracles had happened to prove they were. But now that God had decided not to go with them, the Israelites came to their senses. They mourned and did not put on their makeup. Moses knew this one true and faithful God from the burning bush.

Like the Israelites, we are stiff-necked people. We like controlling our lives and keeping God at bay so we can use Him whenever we need Him. Moses pleaded for the Israelites, and today it's you and I pleading our own cases. Let the Lord know your dependence on Him and that you are not moving and going up without Him. We want Him to lead us with a cloud during the day and with a pillar of fire during the night. Otherwise, how will it be known to the people around us that you and I have found grace in God's sight? We are empty without God, and when we walk alone, we are lost and perish in our sinfulness.

Prayer: We refuse to move from here without You, Lord. Please *"go with us."*

Day 60: **Who Is Listening?**

"So it was, while they conversed and reasoned, that Jesus Himself drew near and went with them" (Luke 24:15 NKJV).

This is one of my very favorite stories in the Bible. Please read the whole text for a better understanding. These two disciples were walking but also engaged in a deep conversation. They were grieving the death of the one who was *"a Prophet mighty in deed and in word, before God and all the people"* (Luke 24:18 NKJV). This is what had filled their hearts, and the overflow is what they said and was recorded. They were His disciples, *"but their eyes were restrained, so they did not know Him"* (Luke 24:16 NKJV). They wondered how Jesus had missed this breaking news of Jesus's death, so they asked him, *"'Are you the only stranger in Jerusalem, and have not known the things that have happened there in the days?'* Then they explained but after a while, they invited Jesus in their house. Jesus came in and when time came, He broke bread and gave them. Then their eyes were opened and they knew it was Jesus. He then vanished from their sight" (Luke 24:31 NKJV).

I can only imagine the mixed emotions the disciples had. Yes, Jesus was risen and "Oh, how did we not recognize Him?" At the same time, they said, *"Did not our heart burn within us while He talked with us on the road, and while He opened scriptures to us?"* (Luke 24:32 NKJV). They got up and returned back to Jerusalem and shared the good news of the risen Christ.

If Jesus appeared, and He restrained our eyes so we didn't recognize Him, what would we say? Would we be ashamed of our conversations and wish we hadn't said this or that? Would we be more sensitive about the boss, friend, relative, or ex and be nicer and choose our words when talking about them? *"Let the words of my mouth, and the meditation of my heart, be acceptable in Your sight, O Lord!"* (Ps. 19:14 NKJV).

Prayer: Help me, oh Lord, to be sensitive when talking about other people.

Day 61: **Strike To Destroy**

> *"The arrow of the LORD's deliverance and the arrow of deliverance from Syria; for you must strike the Syrians at Aphek till you have destroyed them"* (2 Kings 13:17b NKJV).

The time came, and the servant of God, Elisha, was on his deathbed. The king came to see him and *"wept over his face"* (2 Kings 13:14 NKJV). Elisha gave the king simple but powerful instructions that had a lasting impact to the nation of Israel. *"'Open the east window,' the prophet said, and he opened it. Then Elisha said 'Shoot,' and he shot. And he said; 'Strike the ground,' so he struck three times and stopped. And the man of God was angry with him and said, 'You should have struck five or six times, till you had destroyed it!'"* (Please read the whole story.)

What a missed opportunity! This would have been it! The Israelites would have completely destroyed the Syrians. The sad thing is that the prophet died. Maybe if he lived longer, his anger would have subsided, giving the king another chance. It was a one-time anointing.

How many times have you missed opportunities that had a long-time effect over your life? This was a moment of long-term victory for the nation of Israel. They would have peace for many years. Whatever you have to do, do it quickly and do it well, and follow instructions. Don't give up at the count of three. Go a little further: pray, worship, ask, knock, and seek until you get your victory.

Ever seen revolving doors? Once you miss getting in when they revolve, you have to wait until it revolves again. Life is full of revolving doors, and revolving time matters. It can take longer than expected. Don't leave for tomorrow what you can do today. Tomorrow is not promised, and as long as it is day, *"I [we] must do the works of Him who sent Me [us] the night is coming, when no one can work"* (John 9:4–6 NKJV).

Prayer: Father, give me the strength to strike more than three times to have victory in life through faith.

Day 62: **Return**

*"'If you will return, O Israel' says the Lord, 'Return to me' and if you will put your abomination away, out of My sight, then you shall not be **moved**"* (Jer. 4:1 NKJV, emphasis added).

God was talking to His people who, due to their wickedness, had turned to the worship of idols. God was filled with wrath and left the enemy to take them to captivity. *"For you are a holy people to the Lord your God; The Lord your God has chosen you to be a people for Himself, a special treasure above all the people on the face of the earth"* (Deut. 7:6). And to us, who have been purchased by His Son's precious blood, *"I do not pray for these alone but also for those who will believe in Me through their word"* (John 17:20 NKJV).

The Israelites, although they were a chosen people, kept going back and forth in the worship of idols. In His anger, God turned His face away, but when they repented, due to His unfailing love, He would forgive them, giving them yet another chance.

We have the same struggle today. We turn from our loving God, one who saved us from our sinfulness. When the journey becomes very tough, we run for help from the wrong places. Some run to drugs, alcohol, relationships, witchcraft, and so on.

Our call today is from a patient, loving, and merciful God. He knows that we can so easily return to our old sinful ways. He is aware of our weaknesses, and we can easily fall short of His glory. His call is that if we wish to return, RETURN to Him, put away all our abominations, and we shall not be **moved** by the currents of the present age and time.

Prayer: *Help us to "return to Me [You] and I [You] will return to you [us]"* (Mal. 3:7 NKJV).

Day 63: Rivers of Living Waters

"And it shall be that every living thing that moves, wherever the rivers go, will live. There will be a very great multitude of fish, because these waters go there: for they will be healed, and everything will live wherever the river goes" (Ezek. 47:9 NKJV).

Ezekiel was watching this river of God flowing from the altar, and it rose from the ankles to the point that one could swim in it. The river kept flowing, and its banks had many trees growing on both sides, and *"when it reaches the sea its waters are healed"* (Ezek. 47:8 NKJV). Hence, today's Scripture: *"Every living thing that moves, wherever the rivers go, will live. There will be a very great multitude of fish"* (Ezek. 47:9 NKJV).

The river is flowing; it's not stagnant, and for that reason, it carries life in it. It brings with it nutrients from the trees along the banks. When it enters the sea, the water of the sea becomes fresh. So, everything will live where the river goes (Ezek. 47:9 NKJV).

"Fishermen will stand beside the sea . . . and spread nets for the fishermen" (Ezek. 47:10 NKJV). *"He that believes in me as the scripture has said out of his belly shall flow rivers of living water"* (John 7:38 NKJV). I'm challenged by this Scripture and ask myself, what is flowing from my belly? Does the water that comes from me have life in it, or do people perish when they taste it? *"But it's swamps and marshes will not become fresh; they are to be left for salt"* (Ezek. 47:11 NKJV).

Are rivers of living water flowing from your belly, or are you **stagnant** and **salty**? May the Lord help us not be stagnant but start flowing again. May those we encounter have life and health because of the living water flowing from us.

Prayer: Oh, Lord! Let there be rivers of living waters flowing from my belly so that people who interact with me will live again and not perish in their sinfulness.

Day 64: **Good and Bad Figs**

"For I will set my eyes on them for good, and I will bring them back to this land; I will build them and not pull them down, and I will plant them and not pluck them up" (Jer. 24:6 NKJV).

Jeremiah saw a vision of two baskets of figs: one with very good figs and the other one with very bad figs. God explained what that meant, and he said that the very good figs were *"those who are carried away to captive from Judah. whom I have sent out of this place for their own good, into the land of Chaldeans"* (Jer. 24:5 NKJV). It does not make sense for good people to be taken away as captives. If they were very good, why didn't they just stay in their land, where they grew wheat for bread and grapes for wine? Where they kept livestock and offered sacrifices to God at the appointed time? But God had good news for them: *"For I will set my eyes on them for good, and I will bring them back to this land. I will build them and not pull them down and I will build them and not pluck them up"* (Jer. 24:6 NKJV, emphasis added).

This is for those who have grown children or loved ones who have been lost in sins. You showed your children the way to follow, but they fell in sins and are now in captivity. The Lord, through the prophet Jeremiah, said, *"Then I'll give them a heart to know Me, that I am the Lord and they shall be my people and I will be their God. **For they shall return to me** with their whole heart* (Jer. 24:7 NKJV, emphasis added). This is good news to many of us who have gone through a difficult situation with their loved ones.

Captivity, my readers, is not a place of celebration. *"By the rivers of Babylon, there we sat down, yea, we wept when we remembered Zion . . . how shall we sing the Lord's song in a foreign land?"* (Ps. 137 NKJV). But be of good courage, for in due time, **they will return.** Keep trusting and believing, for it shall surely come to pass.

Prayer: As hard as it is, Lord, help me to believe that they shall return to Your ways. They shall be Your people, and You shall be their God.

Day 65: Who Is Like Our God?

"They bear it on their shoulders, they carry it and set it in its place and it stands. From its place it shall not move, though one cries out to it, yet it cannot answer, nor save him out of his trouble" (Isa. 46:7 NKJV).

"*To whom will you liken Me and make Me equal and compare Me, that we should be alike?*" (Isa. 46:5 NKJV) God then continued to give a description of the gods that were made by the hands of men. "*They lavish gold out of the bag . . . they hire a goldsmith, and he makes it a god. They prostrate themselves, yes, they worship. **They bear it on their shoulder, they carry it**" (Isa. 46:6 NKJV, emphasis added). When they cried out to this god, it did not hear them; it had hands but didn't deliver them when they were in trouble; it had legs, but they never moved to come to their rescue; and it had ears, but it didn't hear them when they cried for help.

Praise the Lord our Savior, for He carries us in His arms, each day (Ps. 68:19 NKJV). Hallelujah! He gathers me each day in his arms; he delivers me from all trouble. "*He set my feet up on a rock*" (Ps. 40:2b NKJV).

My reader, this thought and truth should give us great joy and encouragement. We serve a God who is alive! He daily manifests Himself in our lives. Who is like our God? Who can compare to our King of kings? "*He declares the end from the beginning*" (Isa. 46:10 NKJV). He has you and me where He wants us to be. He understands our pain and sorrow. He holds our future in His hands. "*For the Lord your God is He who goes with you, to fight for you, against your enemies to give you victory*" (Deut. 20:4 NKJV). The battle may be so fierce and, at times, we feel like we are losing it, but rest assured that "*the eyes of the Lord are upon the righteous and his eyes are open unto their cry*" (Ps. 34:15 NKJV). Thank you, Jesus!

Prayer: Oh Lord, thank you for carrying me through during times of trouble.

Day 66: **Dry Brook**

"And it will be that you shall drink from the brook, and I will command the ravens to feed you there" (1 Kings 17:4 NKJV).

These are the words of God to his servant Elijah after he had prophesied to Ahab: *"There shall be no dew nor rain these years, except at my word"* (1 Kings 17:1b NKJV). During those years of drought, Elijah was well cared for. He had a constant supply of food. *"And the ravens brought him bread and meat in the morning and bread and meat in the evening: and he drank from the brook"* (1 Kings 17:6 NKJV). Birds that were highly intelligent and carnivorous didn't eat the bread and meat, but they were faithful at the command of the Creator to take and deliver to Elijah bread and meat that were steaming from God's oven.

Due to the prolonged drought, the brook dried up, and God, in his amazing plans over our lives, brought another provision. He sent Elijah to a widow at Zarephath, many of us know the rest of the story: Elijah was provided for, as well as the widow and her household, for the rest of the drought. *"The flour was not used up nor did the jar of oil run dry"* (1 Kings 17:16 NKJV).

If you are like me, there are many times God has provided in miraculous ways. When one brook dries up, He has provided for another way out. What is your need right now? How long have you cried out to God about this issue? Are you discouraged?

There is a God in heaven: *"Look at the birds of the air, for they neither sow nor reap nor gather into barns; yet your heavenly Father feeds them. Are you not of more value than they?"* (Matt. 6:26–34 NKJV). He knows it all! He knows the details of your struggle and understands how you got there. Keep holding on a little longer.

Prayer: Thank you, Lord, for You are still God, and in due time, everything will be beautiful.

Day 67: **The Lord, My Helper**

> *"If the Lord does not help you, where can I find help for you? From the threshing floor or from winepress?"* (2 Kings 6:27 NKJV).

This was a difficult time for the Israelites. The king of Syria and his army had besieged them. *"And there was a great famine in Samaria; and indeed, they besieged it until a donkey's head was sold for eight shekels of silver, and ¼ of a kab of dove droppings for five shekels of silver"* (2 Kings 6:25 NKJV). It was very serious and everyone was affected; the rich who had money could afford a donkey's head or doves droppings. We are not told what the poor did, but we read of this woman who saw the king passing by, and she cried for help. The answer from the king was powerful: *"If the Lord does not help you, where can I find help for you?"* (2 Kings 6:27 NKJV).

The women had eaten a child the previous day, and the following day, the one woman hid her child. What was the king to do? That reminds me of COVID-19; it didn't know any geographical boundaries. Corona went to the poor and rich; it killed people of all walks of life, flooding hospitals with people of all ages. There seemed to be no cure for it; no politician could help, but God!

Many are the times when people turn to the wrong things for help. People turn to relationships that make matters worse. Others become hopeless in life and have no idea where to turn to. Some have gone to the extent of taking their own lives. David said, *"My help comes from the Lord who made heaven and earth"* (Ps. 121:2 NKJV).

Our complete, genuine, and no-strings-attached help only comes from the Lord. Seek His face today and fix your eyes on Him. He will never let you down. He's saying, *"Come to me, all you who labor and are heavy laden and I will give you rest"* (Matt. 11:28 NKJV).

Prayer: Dear Lord, when all hope is gone, it seems so dark, and I cannot make it alone. Help me to trust in You.

Day 68: The Poor and the Fatherless

"Defend the poor and the fatherless; do justice to the afflicted and the needy, deliver the poor and the needy; free them from the hand of the wicked" (Ps. 82:3–4 NKJV).

What a sensitive subject this is! *"For the poor will never cease from the land; therefore, I command you saying, 'you shall open your hand wide to your brother, to your poor and your needy in the land'"* (Deut. 15:11 NKJV). God has a heart for the poor and the needy; that's why we have so many Scriptures addressing this issue. There will never be a time when we don't have the needy among us. We just need to intentionally open our eyes to see them. The needy are not necessarily who need material things; hopelessness, discouragement, being lost in addiction, moral decay, abandonment, rejection, illness, loneliness, and so on leave many people needy and poor in their spirit.

In today's passage, the poor, fatherless, widows, and strangers are specifically mentioned. These are groups of people who are in our midst at all times. These situations are mostly not by choice, and we ask ourselves: Why does God allow these things to happen? Why doesn't He do something?

He is doing something to these brothers and sisters through you and me. He is calling us to defend, do justice, deliver, and free them from the hands of the wicked. *"Open your mouth, judge righteously, and plead the cause of the poor and the needy"* (Prov. 31:9 NKJV).

Do you feel like you have been faithful enough in doing what He has called you to do? Have you been at the forefront of helping these groups of people, or have you been used to fueling the fire that makes life more difficult and unbearable for them?

Prayer: Help me, oh Lord, to be a voice to the voiceless and plead the case of the poor, fatherless, strangers, and the needy.

Day 69: **Ephod**

"And you shall make holy garments for Aaron your brother for glory and beauty" (Exod. 28:2 NKJV).

God gave instructions on how to make an ephod and other priestly garments for Aaron, the high priest, and his sons. It amazes me how detailed God is on this priestly garment. When all the instructions were followed, and the garment was done, it would not only be **glorious,** but it would also be **beautiful.**

God chose colors of the garment and threads. *"They shall take the gold, blue, purple and scarlet thread and the fine linen"* (Exod. 28:5 NKJV). After the garments were glorious and beautiful, *"You shall anoint them, consecrate them and sanctify them; that they may minister to Me as priests"* (Exod. 28:41 NKJV).

In those days, priests went to the holy of holies on behalf of the congregation. Only priests were allowed in that place. They went into the presence of God and made sacrifices on behalf of everyone.

When Jesus said, *"it is finished"* (John 19:28 NKJV) on the cross, the curtain was split, giving us access to the holy of holies. *"Let us therefore come boldly to the throne of grace, that we may obtain mercy and find grace o help in time of need"* (Heb. 4:16 NKJV).

God has a standard for those who go into His presence. *"If therefore you are offering your gift at the altar and there you remember your brother has anything against you be reconciled to your brother and then come and offer your gift"* (Matt. 5:23–24 NKJV). God is looking for that glory and beauty.

Likewise, in the Lord's Prayer, forgiveness is addressed, and when we forgive each other, it's like we have worn a beautiful and glorious garment (the ephod), and with it, we can come before him to offer sacrifices.

Prayer: Lord, help us to wear the right garment during prayer—the garment of reconciliation and forgiveness.

Day 70: **Are You His?**

"I pray for them. I do not pray for the world but for those whom You have given Me. For they are Yours" (John 17:9 NKJV).

This is the only time that Jesus prayed for His disciples. The prayer is powerful and very intimate: *"I do not pray that You should take them out of the world, but that You should keep them from the evil one"* (John 17:15 NKJV). So, we will continue to be in this world, but the evil one shall not have dominion over us. We shall meet challenges like everyone else and maybe more because *"the world has hated them because they are not of this world, just as I am not of the world"* (John 17:14 NKJV). Have you ever been in a difficult situation, and someone sends you a text, saying, "I prayed for you"? Pastors in my church will periodically pray for me and then sign a card and send it in the mail. The card often has a simple but very powerful message: "We prayed for you."

Jesus prayed for His disciples and also said: *"I do not pray for these alone, but also for those who will believe in Me through their word"* (John 17:20 NKJV). Hallelujah! We were prayed for as well. Jesus specifically prayed for a certain group of people, those who believed in Him through His disciples' word.

Be encouraged. The King of the universe has prayed for you because he can identify with your sorrow, pain, rejection, and abandonment. He understands what it means to be lonely, and that's why He took His time before leaving this world to specifically pray for you. And He is not done with us yet. *"He is at the right hand of God, interceding for us"* (Rom. 8:34 NKJV).

Which group do you belong to? The one that He has prayed for, or the other that He calls the world? Believe in Him as Lord and Savior, and you will belong to those He prayed for.

Prayer: Dear Lord, I thank you for praying and interceding for me.

Day 71: Put That In My Account

"If then you count me as a partner, receive him as you would me. But if he has wronged you or owes anything, put that on my account (Phil. 17–18 NKJV).

The book of Philemon has a beautiful account of Paul being in prison. He met this thief, a runaway slave and worthless person. He preached the gospel to him, and the thief gave his life to Christ. This slave's name was Onesimus. Philemon was his master, who was a believer and coworker with Paul.

Paul wrote a letter to Philemon about his slave Onesimus. *"I appeal to you for my son Onesimus, whom I have gotten while in my chains, who once was profitable to you and to me"* (Phil. 10–11 NKJV). How does a runaway slave become profitable to someone he found in chains and the master he had run away from?

"Therefore, if any man be in Christ, he is a new creature: all things are passed away; behold all things are become new" (2 Cor. 5:14–21 NKJV).

Onesimus became a new creature and very dear to Paul. he was being sent back to Philemon, and in his plea, Paul was asking Philemon to receive Onesimus as he would receive him. And if there's anything that he owed, Paul was asking him to put it in his account.

Where do you find yourself in this very interesting story? Is it a child or someone close to you who has run away in sinfulness? Paul said, *"For perhaps he departed for a while for this purpose, that you might receive him forever. No longer a slave [sinner] but more than a slave-a beloved brother"* (Phil. 15-16 NKJV). Are you ready to take back a fugitive who has wronged you or hurt you so much? Like Paul, do you have a disciple you need to advocate for? Are you willing to pay the price for him, anything he owes his master?

Prayer: As hard as it is, Lord, give me a forgiving heart to forgive and take back those who have wronged me. Also, give me a heart like Paul's to preach in chains and bring souls to Christ.

Day 72: Take Up Your Bed and Walk

"Sir, I have no man to put me into the pool when the water is stirred up; but while I am coming, another steps down before me" (John 5:7 NKJV).

There was a pool that had five poaches. *"And there lay a big multitude of sick people; blind, lame, paralyzed waiting for the moving of the water"* (John 5:3 NKJV). The story continues, and it so happened that there was one who had been there for thirty-eight years. When Jesus asked him if he wanted to be well, he had an answer that explained his situation and the reason he had been there for so long. Jesus, passionately and knowing how long this man had been suffering with this infirmity, said to him: *"Rise take up your bed and walk"* (John 5:8 NKJV). It's recorded that the men got well instantly, rose up, took his bed, and walked away.

It concerns me how long this man was lying at the pool. I tend to think that his family or someone used to bring him food and other necessities. I wonder why no one decided to stay there with him, to wait until the water was stirred. I thought of myself and some situations that have caused me pain for so long and relatives and friends that were aware of my situations. They might have come to show sympathy and sometimes provide temporary help, but what I've learned is that only Jesus can do what no one else can. Our Lord delights in doing what is impossible with men.

From what have you been suffering? How long has it taken? There's good news for you. Jesus is passing by, and he's asking, *"Is there anything too hard for me?"* (Jer. 32:27 NKJV). We serve a God who is not only familiar with our problems and circumstances, but He also has a way out. *"No temptation has overtaken you except such as is common to man; but God is faithful, who will not allow you be tempted beyond what you are able, but with temptation will also make the way of escape that you may be able to bear it"* (1 Cor. 10:13 NKJV). Believe it and live!

Prayer: Lord, I want to be well.

Day 73: Blessed Are the Forgiven

"Blessed is he whose transgressions is forgiven, whose sin is covered" (Ps. 32:1 NKJV).

"Why have you despised the commandment of the Lord, to do evil in His sight? You have killed Uriah the Hittite with the sword: you have taken his wife to be your wife" (2 Sam. 12:9 NKJV). This is a very touching story of a deadly act from a king *"The Lord sought for Himself a man after His own heart . . ."* (1 Sam. 13:14 NKJV). In this passage, you will see how easily human beings fall short of the glory of God, how sin attracts other sin.

For David, it started with the lust of the eye, then the lust of the flesh, which ended with killing Uriah to have his wife. It is possible to do something wrong, and when asked, we lie, and that lie calls for another lie, and before someone knows it, they have gone so far in sin.

Not knowing who Nathan was talking about, King David said such a person deserves death penalty. David realized his sin and repented without giving any excuses. He knew that's what he deserved, but God had mercy on him. Though the child born by Bathsheba died, David found peace with God, and he proclaimed, *"Blessed is he whose transgressions is forgiven"* (Ps. 32:1 NKJV).

My brother/sister, what transgression have you done? Is it worse than what David did? Yet, he was forgiven. It is the work of the enemy to entice us to sin and then make you think God will never forgive you. He does not want you to know that Jesus came so we may *"have life, and that (we) may have it more abundantly"* (John 10:10 NKJV). Jesus want to forgive you and set you free. And *"If the Son makes you free, you shall be free indeed"* (John 8:36 NKJV). There is no sin too big that God cannot forgive. *"My little children, these things I write to you, so that you may not sin. And if anyone sins, we have an advocate with the Father, Jesus Christ the righteous"* (1 John 2:1 NKJV).

Prayer: Thank you, Jesus, for the forgiveness of sins.

Day 74: **Shaken Foundations**

"When the foundations of the earth are destroyed, what shall the righteous do?" (Ps. 11:3 NKJV).

The psalmist wrote and asked what would happen if the foundations of the earth were shaken. Have they not been shaken already? Jobs are lost, cars crash, there is loss of loved ones, divorce, unusual diseases, houses are burned to the ground, wars, children rebel, there are shootings every day, and thousands are killed in the wake of other people's sins. What shall the righteous do? Where will you run to?

David's foundations were constantly shaking when Saul chased him in search of his soul. Up the mountains and down in valleys and caves, David ran, looking for a hiding place. He finally came to terms with self: *"In the Lord I put my trust"* (Ps. 11:1 NKJV). It is only in the Lord that he could find a hiding place.

The rain came down, the streams rose, and the winds blew and beat against that house, yet it did not fall because it had its foundations on the rock (Matt. 7:25). Pressure came from above [rain came down], underneath [streams rose], and the side [the wind blew], and they all beat against it, yet IT DID NOT FALL.

Has it ever felt like that in your life, with pressure coming from all sides? Have you ever been overwhelmed by hopelessness? *"Those who trust in the Lord are like Mount Zion, which cannot be moved, but abides forever. As the mountains surround Jerusalem, so the Lord surrounds His people. From this time forth and forever"* (Ps. 125:1–2 NKJV). When our lives are shaken, we will not fall because *"The name of the Lord is a strong tower; the righteous run to it and they are safe"* (Prov. 18:10 NKJV).

Prayer: Thank you, Jesus, for being a sure foundation. When the pressures of life come from all sides, I will stand firm in You.

Day 75: **God Is Enough**

"And He said to me 'son of man, can these bones live?' So, I answered, 'O Lord God, You know'" (Ezek. 37:3 NKJV).

Through his Spirit, God took Ezekiel down to a valley that was full of dry bones. *"Then he **caused** him to pass by them all around and behold there were very many in open valley and indeed they were very dry"* (Ezek. 37:2 NKJV). It was a valley full of hopelessness and despair, and no one in their human mind would see anything else other than dry bones. Only God knew if the dry bones would have life. *"O Lord God, You know"* (Ezek. 37:3b NKJV).

When God told Ezekiel to prophesy, he did. *"So, I prophesied as I was commanded and as I prophesied there was a noise and suddenly rattling and the bones came together bone to bone"* (Ezek. 37:7 NKJV). When the prophet had finished obeying God's instructions, *"there arose an exceedingly great army"* (Ezek. 37:10 NKJV).

There are times when we feel that our situations are like dry bones, and we don't want to deal with them because it seems like a waste of time. We forget that God knows if the situation will ever change. He is such a powerful God, and *"The things which are impossible with men, are possible with God"* (Matt. 18:27 NKJV). What we are going through is not hidden from Him. Hold on a little longer, for He has a better plan, and *"He will perfect that which concerns you"* (Ps. 138:8 NKJV). Our God is enough to make dead situations come to life.

Prayer: Help me *"to trust, and not be afraid"* (Isa. 12:2 NKJV).

Day 76: **Starting Point**

"And the Angel of the Lord appeared to him in a flame of fire from the midst of a bush. So, he looked, and behold, the bush was burning with fire, but the bush was not consumed" (Exod. 3:2 NKJV).

What an experience! Seeing the bush burn and the fire not consuming the bush or spreading would be concerning to anyone. It was God's way of getting Moses's attention, for he said: *"I will now turn aside and see this great sight, why the bush does not burn"* (Exod. 3:3 NKJV). When God saw that he had turned, He immediately called him by name. What followed was a long conversation. When Moses resolved in his heart that he would obey and do as he was commanded, everything changed. He received power and was unstoppable. God proved who He was, and Moses believed in Him.

God revealed Himself to Moses beyond any reasonable doubts. He did miracles to prove that He was the I AM. When the journey became tough, and the children of Israel disobeyed God, Moses always remembered his experience at the burning bush. He remembered his commitment to God.

Do you have a "burning bush" experience? Is there a time in your spiritual life when Jesus proved to you that He was the Son of God? Did you make that decision of letting Him take control of your life? If you did, that was your starting point. Some people are religious and don't have a relationship with the Lord. *"You believe that there is one God. You do well. Even the demons believe and tremble!"* (James 2:19 NKJV). When the journey becomes tough, your "burning bush" experience will remind you of the GREAT I AM and how real He is.

Prayer: Thank you, Lord, for loving me so much that you came down to save me.

Day 77: You Won't Believe This

"For I am going to do something in your days that you would not believe, even if you were told" (Hab. 1:5 NIV).

Have you ever been in a tough situation and wondered where God is? This has happened to me many times. After following Jesus for many years, I would have thought that everything would go well. John the Baptist had a similar question. He sent his disciples to inquire from Jesus: *"Are you the one who is to come, or shall we look for another?"* (Luke 7:19 NKJV). John was in prison and was soon to be beheaded. He thought that if Jesus was the one who was to come, he should use His power to get him out of prison.

In our text today, Habakkuk questioned God concerning Israel. He wondered if God was deaf or had any compassion for His people. In His mercies, and in due time, God answered; *"Behold, I will do a new thing"* (Isa. 43:19 NKJV).

When God is silent and we question His presence, He is actually at work for us. When it is so dark that we can hardly see an inch ahead of us, it is true that if we were told that He is doing a new thing, we would not believe. Do you feel like you are walking *"through the valley of the shadow of death?"* (Ps. 23:4 NKJV). Is the pain you are going through as bad as labor pains? *"He is doing a new thing."* These are your instructions: *"Write the vision, and make it plain on tablets . . . Though it tarries, wait for it because it will surely come"* (Hab. 2:1–3 NKJV).

It might be slow, and it might feel like it is taking forever, but it is for an appointed time. Hold on for a little longer, for it is coming to pass. It doesn't seem like it, but yes! His promises are true, and they will be fulfilled within your lifetime. He has promised to not leave nor forsake you (Heb. 13:5 NKJV).

Prayer: Oh Lord, give me strength to believe that You are doing something new in my life.

Day 78: **True Freedom**

"So she, having been prompted by her mother, said, 'Give me John the Baptist's head here on a platter'" (Matt. 14:8 NKJV).

John the Baptist is the one who was *"the voice of the one crying in the wilderness; make straight the way of the Lord"* (John 1:23 NKJV). His message was to tell people to **repent** in preparation for Jesus. He lived a simple life, wore garments of camel's hair and a leather belt, and his food was locusts and wild honey. He prepared the way of the Lord by preaching and baptizing many after repenting of their sins.

One of those who heard John the Baptist's message was Herod and Herodias, his brother's wife, and he had warned Herod of taking his brother's wife and told him it wasn't right. After dancing before the king, Herodias' daughter was given the head of John on a platter. We wonder, how did she benefit from it? What good came from killing the prophet of God? Herodias thought she had the freedom to do what John the Baptist had pointed out as sin. Did killing him change the fact that she was guilty of being with her husband's brother? Sin remained sin!

The freedom we seek to do what is wrong is not freedom at all. We actually get into deeper sin and guilt. Some children seek to attain a certain age so they can leave home and start life on their own, where they will have "freedom" from their parents. Before they know it, that freedom turns to addiction, sexual immorality, killings, and sometimes they end up in jail. The freedom they got from their parents ended up enslaving them.

Only Jesus gives perfect and eternal freedom. Once you are in Christ Jesus and walk in his ways, you will never fear any authority because Jesus calls for us to obey authority. *"You will be free and free indeed"* and he is promising to give life and life in abundance" (John 10:10 NKJV).

Prayer: Help me, Lord, to always prepare a way for You in my life.

Day 79: **Are You Old Enough to Lead?**

"But when they heard it, they went away one by one, beginning with the older ones" (John 8:9 NKJV).

In our text today, men picked up stones to kill the woman who was caught in adultery. I always wonder where the man involved in the action was. I hope he was not among the crowd of men. As Jesus continued to write on the ground, they became convicted of their own sinfulness. Our text records: *"they went away one by one, beginning with older ones"*.

I've known this text for a long time, but it had never dawned on me that when they dropped the stones, the older ones went first. I felt challenged and asked myself how my reaction on different issues have been. Whether in my house, church, or at the place of work, younger people look up to the elders. Even when they hold positions of power, they still want to hear the input of the older people.

If you are reading this today, know that this text is speaking to you. You may think you are only x years old, but wherever you are in age, there are people younger than you, and they are looking up to you.

Unfortunately, some of us *"gray hairs are sprinkled upon him and he knows it not"* (Hosea 7:9 ESV). It is so sad that one would have gray hair and not know it. So, we end up living careless lives because we do not know our positions.

What you do or say matters a lot. It might mean life or death for a younger person who hears or sees it. May God help us because they are watching us, marking all the things that we do, and hearing all the things we say. May the younger people see the Lord in our actions and hear seasoned words coming out of our mouths.

Prayer: Jesus, help me to know that what comes out of my mouth and my actions matter a lot to the physically and spiritually younger people around me.

Day 80: What Are You Pressing?

"For pressing milk produces curds pressing the nose produces blood and pressing anger produces strife" (Prov. 30:33 ESV).

Sometimes we do things without knowing the outcome. Pressing the nose causes bleeding. I know there are times when people bleed without pressing the nose, but there are less chances that you will press the nose and not see a nosebleed. Pressing anger, on the other hand, produces strife. *"A quick-tempered person does foolish things"* (Prov. 14:17 NIV). "Quick-tempered" means that one is quickly aroused to anger, and Proverbs tells us that such people do foolish things that sometimes make them regret their angry actions. We all become angry at some point in life, but we are advised to *"Be angry, and do not sin. Do not let the sun go down on your wrath"* (Eph. 4:26 NKJV).

Sinning in your anger and letting the sun go down upon your wrath is what is ungodly. The Bible advises us to *"not be hasty in the spirit to be angry, for anger reset in the bosom of fools"* (Eccles. 7:9 NKJV).

If you are hot-tempered, you are not alone. I struggle with anger too, but the Word of God has so much for both of us. Here is a word for us: *"A hot-tempered person stirs up conflict, but the one who is patient calms a quarrel"* (Prov. 15:18 NIV). In your pain, anger, and bitterness, ask God today to help you be patient with that coworker, spouse, child, parent, neighbor, or stranger because you can calm a quarrel. And maybe later, after everything has calmed down, it will be easier to work things out. May God help us so that we don't press anger, for the outcome would be strife.

Prayer: Oh Lord, help me to *"seek peace, and pursue it"* (Ps. 34:14 NKJV).

Day 81: **Alone With God**

"Then Jacob was left alone; and a Man wrestled with him until breaking of day" (Gen. 32:24 NKJV).

Esau, in his hunger, sold his birthright to Jacob, his younger brother, for a bowl of lentils and bread (Gen. 25:30–34). When Isaac, their father, had grown in age and his eyes were dim, he called his son Esau and instructed him to make him a meal so that he would bless him.

With the help of Rebecca, their mother, Jacob killed a young lamb and made a meal for his father, disguising himself as his brother. Jacob received all of his father's blessings, leaving his father Isaac with no blessings for his brother Esau. (Gen. 27:24–29). Esau came shortly after his brother had been blessed and made savory food for his father, only to find that Jacob had come earlier and had received all the blessings. For fear of being killed by his angry brother, Jacob ran away and stayed with his uncle Laban for many years.

The time came for Jacob to return to his people. He took his wives and children and all his possessions. Not knowing what to expect from his brother Esau: *"So, Jacob was greatly afraid and distressed; and he divided the people that were with him, and the herds and camels into two companies"* (Gen. 32:7 NKJV). It was after he sent everyone and all the livestock away that he "was left alone; and a Man wrestled with him until the breaking of day . . . And He blessed him there (Gen. 32:24 NKJV).

Sometimes what you need **is alone time** with God. When life situations are very tough, and you have no idea how to make it through, look for **alone time with God.** Pray in the wildest way and wail in His presence; you can be as loud as you want. Wrestle with God, because it's never in vain to be in His presence, and things are not the same after **alone time with God.** It might mean getting a new name!

Prayer: Help me, oh Lord, to find solace and a hiding place in You.

Day 82: **A Hundredfold**

"Assuredly I say to you, there's no one who has left house or brothers or sisters or father or mother or wife or children or lands, for My sake and the gospel's, who shall not receive a hundredfold now in this time—houses and brothers and sisters and mothers and children and lands with persecution— and the age to come, eternal life" (Mark 10:29–30 NKJV).

How long have you been a Christian? When you committed to following the Lord, were there things you left behind for the sake of the kingdom? I'm sure you did because I did. In our text today, Jesus mentions leaving our close relatives: fathers, mothers, brothers, children, sister, wife, or land. What does that really mean? Does it mean that when we get saved, we disown everyone in our family? Does it mean that we give up land and everything that we possess? The same Bible tells us: *"If anyone does not provide for his own, and especially for those of his household, he has denied the faith and is worse than an unbeliever"* (1 Tim. 5:8 NKJV).

We have an obligation as Christians to care for our own, but if they disown us and persecute us for our faith, we have to choose between them and Christ. If they take from us what we have, for the sake of Christ, Jesus says, *"who shall not receive a hundredfold now in this time . . ."* (Mark 10:30 NKJV). Whatever you lose for the sake of Christ: your time, material things, or relationships, we are promised a hundredfold in the present age and eternal life.

May you be encouraged, seek the Lord, and do the right things, *"for the Lord is a God of justice; blessed are all those who wait for Him"* (Isa. 30:18b NKJV).

Prayer: Lord, I thank you for being just. Thank you for your promise: a hundredfold in the present life and then throughout eternity.

Day 83: **He Cares For You**

"So it was when, I heard these words, that I sat down and wept, and mourned for many days; I was fasting and praying before God of heaven" (Neh. 1:4 NKJV).

Nehemiah had received sad and troubling news about the city of his father's tombs. *"The survivors who are left from captivity in the province are there in great distress and reproach. The wall of Jerusalem is also broken down, and the gates are burned with fire"* (Neh. 1:3 NKJV). When asked by the king what he needed, Nehemiah, without hesitation, clearly spelled his needs out: The king send him to Judah, gave him letters for the governors of the region to help him pass through, and gave a letter to Asaph to give him the resources he needed.

Though the city of Jerusalem was in ruins and the gates were burnt down, those who lived there had no idea how to repair them. The Ammonite officials and Horonite officials would have wanted this situation to remain like that. But God . . .

There are ruins in our lives. Our families are suffering many forms of infirmities. There are addictions, long-suffering ailments, poverty, broken relationships, pain and struggles, divorce, loss of loved ones, and the list goes on. The Word of God encourages us today that God is working it out. There is nothing that is hidden from Him. He will lay that burden on someone who will not sleep, eat, or drink until all is done.

Those ruins that have been there for so long and look like they are the new norm, the Lord is raising a "Nehemiah" who will repair your cities and burnt gates. Keep trusting; keep on believing. At God's appointed time, everything will fall in place..

Prayer: Thank you, Lord, for reminding me that when it is so dark and all hope is gone, You are sovereign and are still working for me. Help me to patiently wait for You.

Day 84: **Praying the Word**

> *"Remember, I pray, the word that you commanded your servant Moses, saying, 'if you are unfaithful, I will scatter you among the nations; but if you return to Me, and keep my commandments and do them . . .'"* (Neh. 1:8 NKJV).

Nehemiah knew that praying **the word** that God had spoken worked! God is just and keeps His promises. Nehemiah reminded God what He had said. Nehemiah *"wept and mourned, for many days; I was fasting and praying before the God of heaven"* (Neh. 1:4 NKJV). He fasted and prayed that God would forgive him and his father's house's sins and also the sins for the children of Israel (Neh. 1:6).

How much of God's promises do you know for this particular situation or problem you are going through? Is there a **word** that you can pray to God with? Nehemiah knew what God had said about the consequences of their sins; they would be scattered to every part of the world, but if they repented, He would forgive and rescue them.

You need to know what is in God's **word** concerning what you are going through! Are there attacks at the place of work that are unprecedented? What is causing that divorce or relational problem in the immediate or extended family? You can pray the **word** of God concerning these problems: *"No weapon formed against you shall prosper, and every tongue which rises against you in judgement You shall condemn.* ***This is the heritage the servants of God.*** *And their righteousness is from Me"* (Isa. 54:17 NKJV, emphasis added). Hallelujah!

As a child of God, you need to know what your Father says about you. Even Satan knows the Scriptures, and he used it to corrupt Jesus (Matt. 4:6 NKJV). How much more will he corrupt you?

Prayer: Dear Lord, help me to hide your Word in my heart. I remind You what You have said concerning me and my situation.

Day 85: **Promise Keeper**

"And the Lord visited Sarah as He had said, and the Lord did for Sarah as He had spoken. For Sarah conceived and bore Abraham a son in his old age, at the set time of which God had spoken to him" (Gen. 21:1–2 NKJV).

"*For My thoughts are not your thoughts, nor are your ways My ways*" (Isa. 58:8 NKJV). I marvel at how true that verse was those days and how true it is today! God promised His friend Abraham [ninety-nine years old] and his wife of ninety years, *"I will make you exceedingly fruitful: and I will make nations of you, and kings shall come from you"* (Gen. 17:6 NKJV). I don't blame them for laughing when God said that. I would have laughed too.

Sarai, who later became Sarah, at the age of seventy-five, decided to help God in His plans. *"Then Sarai, Abram's wife, took Hagar her maid, the Egyptian, and gave her to her husband Abram to be his wife . . . so he went in to Hagar and she conceived"* (Gen. 16:3–4). It is easy to judge Sarai by asking why she did not wait on God's promises, but we find ourselves in the same situation today. Maybe someone will say that God does not audibly speak to us today, but He does in many ways. We read His Word, and He has His servants who preach to us all the time, but when things don't come along fast enough, we feel like we need to hasten them. We forget that God has His own **set time**, and when it comes, He will fulfill what He has purposed to do in our lives.

What happens when we try to help the struggling butterfly out of his cocoon? He dies immediately! Would we wait on God today? *"'For I know the plans I have for you,' declares the Lord, 'plans to prosper you and not to harm you, plans to bring you a hope and a future'"* (Jer. 29:11 NKJV).

Prayer: Lord, help me to be patient to wait for Your set time, for everything will fall in place, and behold, it will be beautiful.

Day 86: **You Are Enough**

"The hand of the Lord came upon me and brought me in the Spirit of the Lord, and set me down in the midst of the valley; and it was full of bones" (Ezek. 37:1 NKJV).

Dear reader, if you consistently do your devotions, you will notice that I am using this Scripture a second time. I tried so much not to, but there is something I need to bring to your attention. I pray that you see how today's text is personalized. Ezekiel is brought through the Spirit to the valley of dry bones. Then, *"He caused me [Ezekiel] to pass all around"* (Ezek. 37:2 NKJV). God could have commanded the bones to come to life, and there would have been a vast army, just like it happened when Ezekiel prophesied. But He chose to work with His servant Ezekiel.

God has found it good to work with you. Out of millions around you, you have found favor with the King of kings. He has invited you to come work alongside Him. He says: *"You are my friends if you do what I command you"* (John 15:14 NKJV). He commanded Ezekiel to prophesy to the dry bones, and he obediently did so, and behold, a vast army arose from that valley.

Today, I want to make this known to you: you are enough. When God wants to use you, He will because you are enough! Do you feel inadequate, not measuring up, and not important? He wants to use you anyway, just the way you are. *"But the people who know their God shall be strong and carry out great exploits"* (Dan. 11:32 NKJV).

Prayer: Forgive me, Lord, for the days that I take in Satan's deception when he tells me I am not enough.

Day 87: **Rest**

*"There remains therefore a **rest** for the people of God"* (Heb. 4:9 NKJV).

After a long day at work, we need some rest. After the chores in the house, we need rest. After working in the field or yard, doing the lawn, and weeding the flowerbeds, we desperately need a rest. God, too, needed rest after creating the heavens and earth and all that is in them. *"And God rested on the seventh day from all His works"* (Heb. 4:4b NKJV).

In Hebrews 4, we learn of a different rest, God's rest. It is the rest that comes from hearing and obeying the word of God. We see two groups of people to whom the word was preached, but they perceived it differently. For one group, what *"they heard did not profit from them"* (Heb. 4:2 NKJV). *"So, I swore in My wrath, they shall not enter My rest"* (Heb. 4:3b NKJV). This is a subject many would want to put aside and just move on with life without thinking of the consequences of their disobedience to the Word of God.

We all desire a good rest after this world's toils and snares of the enemy after fighting a constant battle with Satan. After all the bruises, pain, and hurt we have experienced from being in the battle field, we need good rest at the bosom of our loving Father.

When you read our text today, do you strongly feel that there is rest for you because you are a child of God? *"Today, if you will hear His voice, do not harden your hearts as in the rebellion"* (Ps. 95:7b–8 NKJV).

Prayer: Lord, thank you for paying off my debt on the cross so that I am considered as one who will enter into Your rest.

Day 88: Woman, You Are Loosed

"But when Jesus saw her, He called her to Him and said to her; woman you are loosed from your infirmity" (Luke 13:12 NKJV).

"*And behold, there was a woman who had a spirit of infirmity eighteen years, and was bent over and could in no way raise herself up*" (Luke 13:11 NKJV). I hope you did not miss that—eighteen years! For that long, this woman was suffering from this infirmity. People around her had been used to seeing her in this state, and it looked normal. The Pharisees had gotten used to seeing this woman, and it never bothered them. But Jesus saw her and had mercy on her. He saw the infirmity and did something about it.

The Pharisees burned with fury. How could Jesus do this on the Sabbath? It was okay to them for this woman to wait for the workdays to get healed! But God . . .

You could be suffering for many years, and no one notices. It looks normal to other people. That infirmity does not capture anybody's attention. It seems okay to remain in suffering and pain, to live in poverty, remain in bondage, and be mentally, physically, emotionally, and spiritually abused.

Jesus is able to not only see you, but He will also bring healing. "*The Lord will perfect that which concerns me; Your mercy, O Lord endures forever; Do not forsake the works of Your hands*" (Ps. 138:8 NKJV).

Prayer: Thank you, Jesus, for being the "*the-God-Who-Sees*" (Gen. 16:13 NKJV). You have seen and healed me. I will love and trust in you all of my days.

Day 89: **Four Leprous Men**

"Now there are four leprous men at the entrance of the gate; and they said to one another why are we sitting here until we die?" (2 Kings 7:3 NKJV).

There was a great famine in Samaria, and all the people were desperate and did not know what to do, but the Lord who cares for His people spoke these words through His prophet: *"Tomorrow about this time a sear of fine flour shall be sold a shekel, and two seahs of barley for a shekel at the gate of Samaria"* (2 Kings 7:1 NKJV).

The four outcast lepers who stayed at the gate knew if they went to the city, they would die. If they stayed at the gate, they would die of hunger, and if they went out of the gate, the Syrians would kill them. They chose to go out of the city and hoped they would find something to eat.

God used these outcasts to get the whole city out of the ditch of hunger. As they walked closer to the camp of the Syrians, *"The Lord had caused the army of the Syrians to hear a noise of chariots and the noise of horses-the noise of a great army"* (2 Kings 7:6 NKJV).

Your situation might be the same where you are at a crossroads. You might wonder how you shall ever come out of the situation you are in. May you be reminded that there is a God who is watching over you. He will not let you crash in your circumstances. Somehow, He will let your enemies hear things that are not there for your sake. *"The Lord will cause your enemies who rise against you to be defeated before your face; they shall come out against you one way and flee before you seven ways"* (Deut. 28:7 NKJV).

Prayer: Oh Lord, I do not know how You will work this out, but help me to only believe in You.

Day 90: **The Lord, Our Strong Tower**

"The name of the Lord is a strong tower, the righteous run to it and they are safe" (Prov. 18:10).

Having gone through the pain of losing a loved one, my eyes are open to the mysteries of God. Why does He give and take away? (Job 1:21). When He gives, we rejoice and don't see that beautiful human being leaving us. We earnestly pray and fast for the healing of our loved one, but in our hearts, we selfishly want that family member to continue living with us. Then God, in his wonderful knowledge, answers our prayers in a different way. He heals our loved one eternally. He takes them home where *"God will wipe away every tear from their eyes: there shall be no more death, nor sorrow, nor crying"* (Rev. 21:4 NKJV).

At that very dark moment, He takes away our family member, and our hearts are terribly broken. Even then, we run to Him for emotional, physical, and spiritual strength. We ask Him for the provision of resources.

I can attest that in the case of my family, God came through in a great way. He provided abundantly more than what we could imagine. He brought people to stand with us during that time. Amid pain and trials, He still remains God and worthy of all of our praise.

However, when there is a cloud of sorrow, pain, and shame, we feel like He has abandoned us. That is the time we see God more clearly! It is during the times of thick darkness that we see stars.

King David knew the way to do it: *"Enter into His gates with thanksgiving, and into His courts with praise. Be thankful to Him and bless His name"* (Ps. 100:4 NKJV).

Prayer: Thank you, Lord, for being my strong tower. I will enter your gates with praise.

CPSIA information can be obtained
at www.ICGtesting.com
Printed in the USA
BVHW051419180423
66257 6BV00008B/327